Healthy Diet Plan

DASH Diet and Grain Free Recipes

Alberta Ramos and Shirley Stokes

Copyright © 2013 Alberta Ramos and Shirley Stokes
All rights reserved.

Table of Contents

INTRODUCTION 1

SECTION 1: DASH DIET 6

WHAT IS THE DASH DIET? 7

What Is Hypertension and Why Is It Dangerous? 8

How Does the DASH Diet Work? 9

DASH STUDY DAILY NUTRIENT GOALS 11

DASH DIET GUIDELINES 12

Using DASH for Weight Loss 13

Intuitive Eating with the DASH Diet 13

Making DASH Dieting Easy 14

EXERCISE AND THE DASH DIET 16

RECIPES FOR THE DASH DIET 17

   Appetizers 18
- DASH Spinach Dip 18
- Stuffed Portabella Mushrooms 20
- Crispy Coconut Chicken Fingers 22
- Vegetable Sushi 24
- Fresh Mushroom Quesadillas 26

   Beverages 28
- Peanut Butter and Banana Smoothie 28

No-Booze Margarita 29
Sugar-free Agua Fresca 30
Spicy, Sweet and Tangy Herbal Tea 32
Non-Alcoholic Hurricane Punch 33

Breakfast 34
Chewy Fruit Bars 34
Broiled Almond-Banana Toast 36
DASH-friendly Oatmeal 37
Healthy Homemade Granola 38
Toasted Breakfast Sandwich 40

Main Dishes 42
Simple Grilled Chicken 42
Basic Barbeque "Pork" Chops 43
Miso-Marinated Cod 45
Blackened Beef 47
Feta-ricotta Greek Pizza 49
Chinese Restaurant Ginger Beef 51
Vegetable Medley Pasta Sauce 53
Portabella Mushroom "Burgers" 55

Sides 57
Baked Macaroni and Cheese 57
Spicy Steamed Eggplant with Peanut Sauce 59
Braised Spring Vegetables 61
Rice Pilaf with Saffron 63
Spicy Garlic Green Beans 65

Salads 67
Spicy Tuna Salad 67
Tabbouleh with Tomatoes 68
Edamame Salad 70
Raw Okra Salad 72
Tomato-Zucchini Salad with Eggs 74
Low Cholesterol Potato Salad 76

Soups 78
Nutrient-packed Kale Soup 78
Meatless Lentil Chili 81
Tangy Carrot Curry 83

Cream of Wild Rice Soup with Fennel 85
Hearty Turkey Soup 87

DASH DIET 5-DAY SAMPLE MENU 89

Modifying the 5-Day Meal Plan 92

CONCLUSION 93

SECTION 2: GRAIN FREE COOKING 94

THE PROBLEM OF GRAINS 96

TRANSITIONING TO A GRAIN FREE DIET 98

A QUESTION OF NUTRITIONAL BALANCE 100

GRAIN FREE SHOPPING AND COOKING TIPS............ 101

READING THE RECIPE KEY 103

BREAKFAST 104

No-Grain Granola (GF, P, LC) 104
Fresh Homestyle Beef Sausages (GF, P, LC) 106
Almond Cottage Cheese Pancakes (GF, P*, LC**) 108
Open-faced Apple, Egg and Salmon Sandwich (GF, P, LC) 110
Almond Waffles (GF, P*) 111
Green Eggs (GF, P, LC) 113
Hot Porridge (GF, P, LC) 114
No-Grain Breakfast Burritos (GF, P, LC) 115
Sweet Potato Breakfast Casserole (GF, P, LC) 117

MAIN DISHES 119

Pot Roast with Fresh Vegetables (GF, P, LC) 119
Tropical Tilapia (GF, P) 121

Barbecue Chicken with Grain-free Sauce (GF, P) 123
Zucchini Pasta with Roasted Sweet Potatoes and Coconut Pesto (GF, P) ... 125
American Taco Pie (GF, P, LC) 127
Braised Chicken with Sweet Potatoes and Fennel Bulb (GF, P) 129
Baked Cashew Chicken (GF, P, LC) 131
Savory Braised Duck (GF, P, LC) 133
Stuffed Bell Peppers with Veal (GF, P, LC) 135
No-Rice Pad Thai (GF, P, LC) 137

BAKING AND DESSERTS 139
Almond-coconut Chocolate Chip Cookies (GF, P) 139
Honey-Buttermilk Panna Cotta (GF, P*, LC**) 141
No-Grain Sandwich Bread (GF, P, LC) 143
Banana Coconut Muffins (GF, P, LC) 145
No-flour Chocolate Lava Cake (GF, P) 147
Coconut-vanilla Frozen Dessert (GF, P, LC) 149
Almond Flour Blueberry Muffins (GF, P, LC*) 151
Cinnamon Roll Muffins (GF, P) 153
Almond Biscuits (GF, P, LC) 155
Rye-style Flax Bread (GF, P, LC) 157

SNACKS 159
Homemade Yogurt (GF, P, LC*) 159
Roasted Pumpkin Seeds (GF, P, LC) 161
Coconut Chicken Strips (GF, P, LC) 162
Fruit and Nut-Stuffed Pears (GF, P, LC) 164
Sesame Almond Crackers (GF, P, LC) 166
Cheese Crisps (GF, P*, LC) 168
Chicken Cracklings (GF, P, LC) 170

SALADS, SOUPS AND SIDES 171
Creamy Cauliflower Soup (GF, P, LC) 171
Matzoh Ball Soup (GF, P, LC) 173
Split Pea and Mushroom Soup (GF) 175
Squash Oven Fries (GF, P, LC) 177
Cranberry Steak Salad (GF, P, LC) 178
Spinach and Blood Orange Salad (GF, P) 180
Kale Coleslaw (GF, P, LC) 182
Roasted Winter Squash (GF, P, LC) 184

A 5-DAY GRAIN FREE MEAL PLAN 185

CONCLUSION 188

Introduction

What is a healthy diet plan anyway? It certainly is not a plan that includes any sort of junk food. The definition of junk food is food that has little to no nutritional value. In fact it may be safe to say that junk food is harmful to your health.

Harmful Side Effects of Junk Food

Junk food is not good for you. Period. If your diet consists mainly of junk food or even just portions you are at higher risk for the harmful side effects of consuming junk food. Harmful side effects include: weight gain, obesity, high blood pressure (hypertension), digestive issues, moodiness, depression, high cholesterol, heart disease, muscle and joint issues, and even a sluggish immune system.

Let's talk about the latter - a sluggish immune system. This is reason number one for most of the issues listed because if the immune system is weak it cannot sufficiently fight off infections. Infections can set in and we become sickly and weak. Our body cannot handle the food so it sticks around and forms into fat. Our digestive system becomes sluggish. We may have toxins build up as a result of that. How do we remedy this? With a diet change, of course.

Dieting Should Be a Lifestyle Change

When you go on a diet, you do so for health reasons. Or you may go on a diet for cosmetic reasons (to lose weight, to fit into "those" jeans, or that dress, or whatever the case may be. Some people may go on a diet for specific health reasons, such as to help lower high blood pressure. Regardless, if you find yourself in need of a diet whether it is to help you fit into smaller clothing or to help you resolve a health issue, you should consider it a permanent lifestyle change. Making it a permanent change will help to avoid the same pitfalls with your health. Going back to the original way you ate will only put your health right back where it was with weight gain, health issues, etc.

Succeeding with a New Diet

Both the DASH diet and the grain free diet plans offer healthy food choices. You will find if you stick with these diets, you will feel better and be much healthier for it. But to succeed you must go past the point of failure that so many others fall prey to when dieting. That is busting the junk food addiction. A food addiction is a tough and real addiction much like being addicted to alcohol or cigarettes. While you can stop suddenly and go on the diet and hope for success if you have a true addiction you will suffer from withdrawals, much like a person would if they are addicted to the alcohol and cigarettes. It helps to go through a weaning process. It helps to keep the withdrawal symptoms to a lower level and gives you a greater chance at success. Here are the steps to a proper weaning from junk food.

Withdrawals from junk food may include headaches, moodiness, lethargy or nervousness, lack of energy, and most certainly intense craving. These are very unpleasant and any of these will cause a person to want to give up on dieting just stopping the withdrawals. Weaning slowly helps to keep these symptoms manageable.

Take the weaning more slow to succeed. It takes the body about three weeks to break a habit. If you try to break it faster, you run the risk of failing with the diet. If you break the bad food habits before you start the diet you will have a greater chance at making the lifestyle change permanent. There are a couple of ways to break the bad food habits.

The first way is to take the full three weeks and slowly replace each time you wish to eat junk food with a healthier choice, such as a hand full of nuts or a piece of fresh fruit. It may be helpful if you keep a food journal for about a week so you know for sure how much junk food you eat. Every three days or so stop eating take away one instance of eating junk food and replace it with a nutritious snack. By the time you reach three weeks you will have completely weaned from all the junk food and should not have to face the unpleasant withdrawal symptoms. You may notice a craving once in a while, but your body will start to enjoy the more nutritious foods instead. You may reach a day where you will no longer care if you eat junk food or not.

Another way to wean from junk food is to do a set elimination of eating it. For the first five days allow yourself to eat junk food three times a day (for snacks or desserts). The next five days change it to eating junk food only two times a day. For the third five days only eat it once a day. For the fourth five days eat junk food once every other day. By the end of this you should be weaned. If you find you still have issues try to "reward" yourself once a weekend with "one" snack of junk food.

Choose whichever way you wish to wean from junk food. It is advisable to go ahead and go on the DASH and grain free diets while you are weaning, using the recipes to create snacks to replace the junk food.

Disclaimer

Always seek the advice and counsel of your own health care provider before starting any new diet routine. The amount of success derived from any diet plan depends on you, on what you do to follow the diet and how you stick with it. Of course, diet is further helped with a good exercise routine, so ask your health care provider about physical activity. Eating healthy may help to maintain healthy blood pressure levels, cholesterol levels, and a manageable healthy weight.

Section 1: DASH Diet

The DASH Diet is an important strategy for anyone who wants to lower their blood pressure and improve their overall health without dealing with risky medications and their side effects. This simple diet focuses on low fat, low cholesterol foods and natural ingredients, making it inexpensive and easy to follow. Plus, you'll be surprised by how delicious heart healthy foods can be. If you've been warned about the possible dangers of high blood pressure and a normal North American diet, it's time to make some changes.

The recipes contained in this book don't encompass the entire range of DASH diet options, but they will give you an idea of how you can change your favorite foods to fit the diet plan. In general, they focus on reducing the fat, cholesterol and refined carbohydrates in a dish without losing out on flavor. If you've experienced too many flavorless health foods, these recipes could be the solution that you've been hoping for.

What Is the DASH Diet?

DASH is a term that stands for "Dietary Approaches to Stop Hypertension." It is designed to be a lifestyle change for people who want to treat or prevent hypertension, also known as high blood pressure. The diet is based on studies originally performed by the US National Institutes of Health that examined three different dietary plans and their effects on blood pressure. The result is a plan that focuses on increased consumption of plant foods such as nuts, beans, low fat dairy products, vegetables and fruit.

This diet plan is recommended by the National Heart, Lung and Blood Institute for anyone who wants to decrease their blood pressure and improve heart health. In studies performed on the diet, people who followed it showed a systolic blood pressure reduction of 6mm Hg, as well as a diastolic blood pressure reduction of 3 mm Hg in patients who had tested in the high-normal range, also called pre-hypertension. In patients who had existing hypertension, the diet caused reductions of 11 mm Hg and 6 mm Hg respectively, with no change in body weight. While it was not designed for weight loss, the DASH diet's focus on lower calorie, healthier foods does make it a viable choice for people who want to reduce their body fat levels.

What Is Hypertension and Why Is It Dangerous?

Hypertension, or high blood pressure, refers to the force your blood puts on the walls of your arteries. Doctors measure it in millimeters of mercury, or mm Hg, and record it as two different numbers. They measure both the systolic blood pressure, or the pressure when your heart is beating, and the diastolic blood pressure, or the pressure between beats. A person's blood pressure can rise and fall over the course of a given day, but continued high levels can be very dangerous to your health.

When your blood flows with a lot of force, it can damage the veins and arteries, as well as organs like the eyes, heart, kidneys and brain. Most people who develop high blood pressure have difficulty lowering it. Left uncontrolled, this condition can lead to blindness, kidney and heart disease, and even stroke. About one in three people have high blood pressure, but many aren't aware of the problem.

Many doctors and patients turn to medication at the

first sign of high blood pressure, but this technique might not be the right one for you. Many blood pressure treatments have dehydrating effects. Others can induce depression or extreme tiredness. The very low blood pressure that is caused by some drugs can also result in severe dizziness and a tingling feeling in your fingers and toes. In more serious cases, these drugs can cause insomnia, pain in the feet, weakness and leg cramps, or an irregular heartbeat. That's a lot of risk to take when you could address the problem through less intrusive methods like diet and exercise.

How Does the DASH Diet Work?

The DASH diet provides an alternative to conventional, drug-based methods of controlling blood pressure. It is designed to help you maintain a healthy weight with moderate levels of physical activity. It focuses on reducing sodium levels, which have been shown to elevate blood pressure in some people. It also includes decreased levels of saturated fat and cholesterol, which contribute to narrowing of the arteries and can make it hard for blood to cycle properly.

Over time, this diet can help patients who have high blood pressure lower their levels and reduce their medication requirements. In some cases, it can even allow you to discontinue use of medication entirely. It is important to change your dosages only on the recommendation of a doctor, however. Don't stop using your high blood pressure medicine just because you've started using the DASH diet.

DASH Study Daily Nutrient Goals

The studies used to formulate the DASH diet set a few standard daily nutrient goals, which are also used in the main plan. Following this diet means trying to keep your total fat intake to about 27 percent of your daily calories. Saturated fat should make up only about 6 percent of your calories, however. The DASH diet is relatively high in carbohydrates, which should make up about 55 percent of your daily calorie intake, but most of the carbohydrates you eat should be complex ones, rather than those derived from white flour and sugar.

The DASH diet also recommends trying to keep your daily cholesterol intake below 150 milligrams. The original studies aimed for a sodium intake of 2,300 milligrams or less, but more recent research suggests that 1,500 milligrams or less is even better for reducing blood pressure. It's a good idea to get at least 30 g of fiber and 1,250 milligrams of calcium each day while on this diet, as well.

DASH Diet Guidelines

All those number can be hard to understand, so the researchers who wrote the DASH diet plan broke it down into clearer recommendations. They suggest eating six to eight servings of whole grain per day, four to five servings of vegetables, and four to five servings of fruit. Consuming two to three servings of low fat dairy products provides protein and calcium. If you eat meat, aim to consume six or fewer one-ounce servings of lean meat, poultry or fish per day. Vegetarians can substitute an egg for one serving of meat.

The DASH diet guidelines recommend consuming four to five servings of nuts, legumes and seeds per week, though vegetarians should increase these to replace meat. Fats and oils should be kept to a relative minimum of two to three servings per day. This includes, mayonnaise, margarine and salad dressings. Sweets need to be eaten in moderation; the DASH diet recommends having five low-fat servings or fewer every week. Very active people can increase servings of grain, fruits and vegetables, low fat dairy and lean meat to help support their higher metabolisms.

Using DASH for Weight Loss

The DASH diet wasn't originally designed to help people lose weight, but it can be adapted to help you maintain a healthier weight and reduce your risk of high blood pressure. Doctors recommend simply using the lower calorie recommendations for the diet to cut back your energy intake. Eat a little less than you normally would and focus on getting about 30 to 60 minutes of regular physical activity, like walking or swimming, every day. Your weight may not decrease dramatically, but it should drop slowly over a longer period of time. Experts recommend this kind of loss because it is the most likely to be permanent.

Intuitive Eating with the DASH Diet

While many people like to start out counting their calories to ensure they're getting the right level of nutrition on the DASH diet, this doesn't work for everyone. If you have trouble with calorie counting, or if you've been on the diet long enough to know your choices are good ones, it might be time to look at intuitive eating. This technique involves paying attention to the signals your body is sending. When you've mastered intuitive eating, you'll provide food when your body is hungry, stop eating when it sends signals of fullness, and avoid snacking for emotional reasons or out of boredom. This method can be very helpful for people who tend to have trouble with more mathematical techniques, but it does take some practice.

Intuitive eating is compatible with the DASH diet from the beginning, but you'll need to modify your strategy a little bit. Start out by focusing on the low calorie foods that are acceptable on this diet. That means consuming more fruit and raw, non-starchy vegetables while eating more calorically-dense foods in small amounts. Even if you have a craving for nuts, beef or cheese, try having just a few bites to begin with. You may be able to conquer your craving quickly without overeating.

Making DASH Dieting Easy

The transition period between a normal North American diet and the DASH technique can be a rocky one, especially if you don't know how to find tasty snacks or eat at your favorite restaurants. Make things simpler by keeping pre-cut fresh fruit, vegetables and low-calorie dairy snacks in your refrigerator at all times. That way, when you want to grab something simple, they'll be right at your fingertips.

Make eating out on the DASH diet easier by turning the menu into a treasure hunt. You may be surprised by how many healthy foods you can find. Most restaurants now offer a veggie burger instead of a beef burger. You may also be able to choose steamed vegetables or fresh fruit rather than French fries or onion rings. Choose a garden salad with a light oil and vinegar dressing in restaurants that don't offer many vegetable options, and be sure to take part of your meal home. You'll find eating out on the DASH diet much simpler than you expected.

Last, but not least, practice sneaking DASH foods into your ordinary meals. It's easy to add cucumber slices, shredded cabbage or carrots to an ordinary sandwich. If you usually consume tea or coffee, add a full glass of skim milk to it to boost protein without increasing your cholesterol. Vegetable broths and fruit purees provide a great way to ensure you're getting all your fruits and veggies: just drink them!

Exercise and the DASH Diet

The DASH diet works well on its own, but when paired with exercise, it has considerably better effects. In one study of 124 men and women over the age of 50, 30 minutes of aerobic exercise three times per week lower blood pressure and weight much more quickly than diet alone. If you need to make lifestyle changes in order to improve your blood pressure and reduce your BMI, adding light to moderate physical activity is the best way to do it.

The process is very simple. Just add a half hour of swimming, walking or other activity to your day at least three times per week. The workout doesn't need to be severe. In fact, you should be able to hold a conversation while you're getting your exercise. Try to recruit a workout buddy to help keep you on track and develop healthy habits. You'll soon be feeling lighter and more energetic. You'll even develop more stamina, making it easier to stay active.

Recipes for the DASH Diet

These recipes are adapted from books and online sources. They range from very simple to multi-step preparations for fancier occasions, but you don't have to be a master chef to prepare them. While several of them rely on slightly unusual ingredients, you should be able to find these at many standard grocery stores. Consider checking the ethnic or natural foods section for low-sodium soy sauce, chili paste and other less common ingredients. The extra flavor they give to your meals makes it worthwhile to seek these foods out.

You don't have to jump straight into preparing just DASH diet recipes, either. You can incorporate a few of these dishes into your normal routine, increasing them until you're eating healthy all week long. That's what makes the DASH diet such a good idea. It helps you make healthy decisions and incorporate them into your life without having to turn your normal way of eating upside down. If you care about the health of your heart, arteries and brain, it may be time to try out some of these great DASH recipes. In just a little while, you won't know how you ever lived without them.

Appetizers

DASH Spinach Dip

This cheesy dip eliminates the cholesterol-laden cream cheese and full-fat sour cream normally used in spinach dips, substituting velvety Great Northern beans and low fat dairy. Instead of heavily-salted ingredients, it relies on flavorful herbs and garlic to add interest. The result is a creamy dip that doesn't taste like health food. It makes a great choice for parties and goes well with sliced vegetables or warm, crusty bread.

Ingredients

2 pounds fresh spinach or 3 packages frozen spinach
1 pound or one can cooked Great Northern beans
½ cup low fat sour cream
2 tablespoons Parmesan cheese
2 tablespoons fresh parsley
1 tablespoon fresh basil
2 teaspoons black pepper
2 cloves fresh garlic

Wash and drain the fresh spinach or thaw and drain if you are using frozen products. Drain the beans and mash or puree until smooth. Combine all ingredients and stir until well combined, then pour into an oven-safe dish. Bake at 350 degrees Fahrenheit for about 30 minutes or until the mixture is hot throughout and bubbly.

Stuffed Portabella Mushrooms

Stuffed mushrooms are a classic appetizer, but they too-frequently contain cholesterol-packed bacon, cream cheese, eggs and other health-hazard ingredients. This version uses fresh spinach combined with garlic, tarragon and strongly-flavored cheese to provide excitement without the fat. The make-ahead element of these stuffed mushrooms means they're the perfect last-minute choice when you have company or just don't want to spend too much time in the kitchen

Ingredients

4 large portabella mushrooms
1 cup fresh or frozen spinach
4 teaspoons grated Parmesan cheese
1 tablespoon fresh tarragon
2 teaspoons olive oil
2 cloves fresh garlic
½ teaspoon black pepper

Crush the garlic and remove the stems from the portabella mushrooms. Chop the stems finely. Drain the spinach thoroughly. Heat 1 teaspoon of olive oil over medium-high heat in a heavy pan and sauté the garlic, pepper and tarragon for one minute. Add the mushroom stems and spinach leaves to the pan, sautéing 3 to 4 minutes or until stems are tender. Remove and place in a bowl. Add remaining 1 teaspoon of olive oil to the pan and place the mushrooms in the pan, cap-side down. Saute for 3 minutes without stirring or turning.

Flip the caps, cover, and reduce heat to low for another 2 minutes. Remove and place the caps on a foil-lined baking sheet with the gills facing up. Fill each mushroom with ¼ of the spinach mixture. Top with Parmesan cheese. If you are making the recipe ahead, cover the sheet with plastic wrap and place it in the refrigerator or freezer until ready to serve. Otherwise, place the mushrooms on a rack 6 inches below your broiler and cook for 3 to 4 minutes, until the cheese has just browned.

Crispy Coconut Chicken Fingers

Coconut shrimp is a perennial favorite, but it's also loaded with saturated fat and cholesterol. This healthier alternative uses chicken thighs to offer just as much flavor in a better-for-you package. Combined with the sweet and spicy dipping sauce, this recipe will be a hit at your next party. Vegetarians and vegans can also enjoy this dish; just substitute tempeh for the chicken and egg replacement powder for the egg white as preferred.

Ingredients

½ pound boneless, skinless chicken thighs
¼ cup no-sodium bread crumbs
¼ cup unsweetened coconut flakes
1 teaspoon powdered garlic
1 egg white
¼ teaspoon black pepper
Dipping Sauce
2 tablespoons orange marmalade
1 ½ teaspoons rice vinegar or lemon juice
¼ teaspoon cayenne pepper

Wash the chicken and pat it dry. Slice into 20 individual bite-sized pieces. Combine the bread crumbs, coconut, garlic and black pepper in a small bowl. Beat egg white thoroughly. Dip each piece of chicken into the egg, then roll in the bread crumb mixture. Place on a lightly-oiled baking sheet and bake at 425 degrees for 10 minutes. Flip each piece, then return the sheet to the oven for another 10 minutes.

Combine all sauce ingredients in a small bowl and stir to combine. Arrange the chicken bites on a platter around the bowl of sauce and serve right away.

Vegetable Sushi

When you mention sushi, most people assume raw fish or eggs will be involved, but the term "sushi" actually refers to the slightly sour rice. You can top this delicate Japanese food with all kinds of ingredients, including fresh and colorful vegetables. Use brown rice to add more fiber and a nutty flavor. You can mix and match the vegetables in this recipe, making it an excellent choice to use up leftovers.

Ingredients

1 cup short grain brown rice
1 1/2 cups water
1 tablespoon plain rice vinegar
1 package sushi nori seaweed sheets
Vegetables
steamed or roasted asparagus spears
avocado
roasted beets
fresh cucumber strips
pickled daikon or radish
shredded kale
roasted sweet potatoes
roasted kale
fresh or sautéed mushrooms

thin slices of tomato

Place the brown rice in a pan or rice cooker brown and rinse until the water runs clear. Drain and add 1 ½ cups of water. Cook until the rice is tender. Sprinkle with vinegar and add salt substitute to taste. Stir with a wide, flat spoon or a rice paddle and allow the mixture to cool.

To assemble, place one sheet of nori on a bamboo sushi mat. Spoon approximately ½ cup of the cooked rice mixture in a thin layer across the whole piece of nori. Place shredded kale, asparagus stalks, cucumber strips or other vegetables on top of the rice, then roll the seaweed over the vegetables and into a long log, using the mat to keep it intact. Place the finished roll seam-side-down on a cutting board and slice into pieces with a very sharp knife. Serve immediately with pickled ginger, low sodium soy sauce, horseradish or sesame seeds.

Fresh Mushroom Quesadillas

Mushroom quesadillas are a popular dish in Mexico, where they are referred to as quesadillas de hongo. Unlike processed American versions of Hispanic cuisine, this dish is light and healthy without being dull or flavorless. Say goodbye to fatty, uniform Mexican fast food and hello to healthy flavor with these spicy but savory tortillas.

Ingredients

1 pound fresh mushrooms
1 medium onion
1 cup shredded Swiss cheese
¼ cup low fat sour cream
3 cloves garlic
2 tablespoons fresh cilantro
1 fresh jalapeno pepper
1 teaspoon olive oil
1 package low sodium, whole grain flour or corn tortillas

Finely chop mushrooms, onion, jalapeno, cilantro and garlic. Heat 1 teaspoon of olive oil in a heavy pan over medium heat and sauté the alliums and mushrooms for about 10 minutes, or until tender and lightly browned. Season with black pepper to taste. Heat a large skillet to medium-low and place a single tortilla on the surface, flipping to warm throughout. Sprinkle with cheese, chopped jalapeno and cilantro. Allow the cheese to melt, then spoon on a small amount of the mushroom mixture. Add a second tortilla and flip the entire quesadilla over. Remove to a plate to cool and repeat until you have used all the cheese and mushroom mixture. Slice each quesadilla into quarters or eighths, depending on the size of your tortilla. Serve warm with low fat sour cream.

Beverages

Peanut Butter and Banana Smoothie

Whether you'd like to enjoy a smoothie for breakfast, dessert or a between-meal treat, this one is a great choice. The banana provides plenty of natural sweetness, while the peanut butter offers monounsaturated "healthy" fats and protein. Combined with non-fat milk, this could be the perfect pick me up when you're feeling tired. Vegans can substitute unsweetened soy or almond milk.

Ingredients

1 cup skim milk
1 medium banana
1 tablespoon creamy natural peanut butter, unsalted

Peel and slice the banana. Place in a blender or food processor and add the milk and peanut butter. Process until completely smooth. For a more milkshake-like version, freeze the banana before blending.

No-Booze Margarita

Most people on the DASH diet need to take alcohol in moderation, while some need to eschew it completely. This tasty beverage offers the same overall flavor as a margarita, but without the alcohol. That means you can drink it at any time!

Ingredients

2 cups ice
½ cup lime juice
2 tablespoons simple syrup
Sliced limes for garnish
Simple Syrup (makes 6 tablespoons):
¼ cup raw sugar
¼ cup water

Combine the water and sugar in a small saucepan over medium heat, stirring until the sugar has dissolved completely. Remove to a sealed container and refrigerate for up to a week.

Combine syrup, ice and lime juice in a blender or powerful food processor. Process until a smooth slush has formed. Pour into a chilled glass and garnish with lime slices.

Sugar-free Agua Fresca

Aguas fresca, sweet non-carbonated beverages popular in Mexico and the southeastern US, can be a refreshing choice for hot days. Unfortunately, most of these drinks contain large quantities of white refined sugar. This variation uses fresh fruit to provide the sweetness, making it a much healthier and lower-calorie option you can enjoy more often.

Ingredients

3 pounds watermelon
½ cup unsweetened cranberry juice
½ cup apple juice
¼ cup lime juice
1 lime

Remove the seeds and rind from the watermelon, cutting it into fine dice. Place it in a food processor or blender and process until a smooth puree is produced. Sieve this puree to remove the excess pulp, yielding a clear, delicious juice. Cut the lime into thin slices. In a large pitcher, combine the watermelon juice, cranberry juice, apple juice and lime juice. Stir to combine completely. The mixture may be slightly cloudy, but it will taste delicious when refrigerated and garnished with a slice of fresh lime.

Spicy, Sweet and Tangy Herbal Tea

Technically a tisane, because no tea leaves are involved in its brewing, this drink can be served either warm or chilled. It uses only natural, unprocessed sweeteners, making it an excellent alternative to sodas and conventional iced tea beverages.

Ingredients

1 ½ quarts water
½ cup fresh mint
1/3 cup lemon juice
3/8 cup strongly-flavored honey
4 tablespoons fresh ginger
1 medium lemon

Peel and chop the ginger. Slice the lemon thinly into rounds. Combine the ginger, water and lemon juice in a saucepan and bring to a boil over high heat. Reduce to low and allow to simmer for 5 minutes. Add the mint, remove from heat entirely, and allow to steep for 5 to 8 minutes. Use a fine sieve to remove the mint leaves and ginger, which can be discarded after use. Stir in the honey and serve warm or cold with a lemon slice floating on top.

Non-Alcoholic Hurricane Punch

Traditionally made with rum, this beverage is a great choice to add lots of vitamin C and other antioxidants to your diet. When made with ice, it becomes a delicious frosty drink that's perfect for a hot summer day.

Ingredients

2 cups or 1 can fresh unsweetened pineapple
1 orange
1 lemon
1 lime
½ cup unsweetened cranberry juice
1 cup ice (optional)

Peel the citrus fruit and set aside. Chop the pineapple roughly into chunks and combine in a blender with the cranberry juice and citrus. Add the ice if you are using it and process until the mixture is a smooth liquid or frosty puree. Serve in tall glasses with a spoon for the icy version.

Breakfast

Chewy Fruit Bars

This simple bar is sweet and hearty, making it the perfect choice for breakfast on the go. Unlike many ordinary granola bars, it's not high in fats or refined sugars, however. Natural ingredients such as multigrain cereal and bran help keep the glycemic index low, while walnuts, dried fruit and almond butter provide the energy your body needs to keep going. Enjoy these bars as a quick snack or even a light dessert in a pinch.

2 cups dry whole grain hot cereal
1 cup bran flakes cereal
¾ cup honey
¾ cup low salt almond butter
½ cup non-fat dry milk
½ cup dried apricot pieces
½ cup dried cranberries
½ cup walnut pieces
1 tablespoon canola or light olive oil
1 tablespoon vanilla extract

In a large bowl, combine cereals, nuts, dried fruit and dry milk. Place almond butter, honey and oil in a small saucepan and heat to medium-low, stirring constantly. Allow mixture to bubble, then remove the pan from the heat and add vanilla extract. Pour this mixture over the fruit and cereal, stirring until completely combined. Grease a baking pan with canola oil or line it with parchment paper. Spread the mixture into the pan, patting it down tightly. Bake for 20 minutes at 325 degrees and set aside to cool on a rack for 20 minutes or until firm. Cut into 12 pieces and store in an air-tight container at room temperature.

Broiled Almond-Banana Toast

Bananas are a classic breakfast ingredient, but on their own they tend to be carbohydrate-heavy and unsatisfying. That's why this morning treat pairs fresh banana with fiber-rich whole grain toast and protein-packed almond butter. Putting the finished product under the broiler caramelizes the natural sugars in the banana, producing a delicious, gooey result that you'll also enjoy as a snack.

Ingredients

2 slices whole grain bread
2 tablespoons smooth almond butter
1 small banana
ground cinnamon and nutmeg to taste

Toast the bread and arrange it on an oven-safe plate or a small baking sheet. Spread each slice with 1 tablespoon of almond butter. Slice the banana into rounds of medium thickness and arrange them on top of the almond butter. Sprinkle the surface with cinnamon and nutmeg, then place under the broiler for 2 to 3 minutes, or until the almond butter melts slightly and the bananas begin to brown. Allow to cool and eat with your fingers, or dig in right away with a fork.

DASH-friendly Oatmeal

Oatmeal naturally has properties that make it good for your heart, but many commercial instant products contain large amounts of sugar, sodium and other unhealthy ingredients. If you love a hot, hearty bowl of oats in the morning, this low-cholesterol, salt-free option will satisfy you without cutting back on taste. Fresh fruit and nuts add to the oatmeal's flavor and nutrition profile, making this a breakfast recipe you're sure to love. Try it out on a cold winter morning.

Ingredients

1 ½ cups unsweetened almond milk
1 cup old fashioned rolled oats
¾ cup mixed berries or other chopped fruit
1/8 cup whole pecans
¼ teaspoon vanilla extract
Cinnamon to taste

Combine the almond milk and vanilla in a small sauce pan over medium-high heat. Bring to a gentle simmer and add the oats. Cook, stirring occasionally, for about 5 minutes or until almost all the liquid has been absorbed. Stir in the fruit and serve topped with pecans and cinnamon.

Healthy Homemade Granola

Traditional granolas are full of healthy ingredients such as whole grains, nuts and fruit, but they tend to be heavy on the fat, salt and added sugar. The situation gets worse in the case of some packaged granolas, which add preservatives and other artificial ingredients. This homemade granola recipe is nutritionally dense and concentrates on healthy fats and natural, relatively unrefined sources of sugar. Flax seeds add an extra omega-3 punch, making this recipe a great way to start your day.

Ingredients

3 cups old-fashioned rolled oats
1 cup sliced almonds
1 cup raisins or dried cranberries
4 tablespoons flax seed
¼ cup raw sugar
1/4 cup honey
¼ cup sunflower or canola oil
½ teaspoon vanilla extract
½ teaspoon ground sugar
½ teaspoon allspice
½ teaspoon ground ginger

Combine the oats, almonds, flax, spices and sugar in a large bowl, mixing thoroughly. In a separate bowl combine the honey, oil and vanilla extract. Pour the wet ingredient mixture into the dry ingredients, mixing with a spatula as you pour. Stir until the dry mixture is wet throughout. Lightly grease one to two cookie sheets with sunflower oil or another monounsaturated fat. Pour the wet granola into the pans, patting it into place if necessary. Bake in a 250 degree Fahrenheit oven for 90 minutes or until dry and lightly browned, stirring every 15 minutes. Break up chunks of granola as you stir to create the appropriate consistency. Allow the mixture to cool, then combine with the dried fruit and store in an air-tight container.

Toasted Breakfast Sandwich

Not every DASH-friendly breakfast recipe is sweet. There are also plenty of savory options that combine fresh vegetables with low-sodium, low-cholesterol proteins for a heartier start to your day. If you love eggs for breakfast, this recipe will help you enjoy them without the heart risk associated with large amounts of egg yolk. Flavorful mustard and tomatoes keep the open-faced sandwich interesting, so you won't miss the fat.

Ingredients

2 egg whites
½ cup fresh spinach leaves
1 slice whole grain bread
1 small tomato
1 ½ teaspoons olive oil
1 teaspoon prepared brown mustard
½ ounce slice reduced-fat cheddar cheese
Black pepper and paprika to taste

In a small pan, heat the olive oil to medium-high. Beat the egg whites and add to the hot oil, scrambling them until completely solid. Add the spinach and heat until wilted. Spread the mustard onto the bread and place it on an oven-safe plate or baking sheet. Arrange tomato slices on top of the mustard, then top with the egg mixture and thinly-sliced cheddar cheese. Sprinkle with black pepper and sharp paprika to taste. Bake in an oven or toaster oven at 400 degrees Fahrenheit until the bread is crisp and the cheese is melted and slightly browned.

Main Dishes

Simple Grilled Chicken

This basic chicken dish is easy to make on any outdoor grill. It combines the low cholesterol and white meat of bone-in chicken breasts with flavorful garlic and spices. The finished product is crisp, golden brown and caramelized for an intense flavor. You won't miss the extra fat!

Ingredients

4 bone-in chicken breasts with skin
2 cloves garlic
salt-free herb seasoning mix

Heat a gas or charcoal grill to medium heat. Fold non-stick aluminum foil into a boat shape for each chicken breast. Cut the garlic cloves in half and rub the cut surfaces over the skin of the chicken breasts. Sprinkle with seasoning mix to taste and place the chicken breasts in the boats, skin side down. Grill for 45 minutes or until the center reaches 160 degrees Fahrenheit, turning the chicken once every 10 to 15 minutes.

Basic Barbeque "Pork" Chops

Barbecued pork may sound unhealthy and decadent, but you can substitute other meats to make your favorite pork recipes compatible with the DASH diet. This recipe uses "chops" of boneless chicken thighs, since the dark meat provides similar flavor intensity to that of lean pork. Just make sure you don't overcook it, as the meat can easily dry out with too much heat. Add a fresh salad and this dish is ready to make a complete meal!

1 ½ pounds boneless chicken thighs
10 ounces low sodium condensed tomato soup
3 tablespoons red wine vinegar
2 tablespoons low sodium Worcestershire sauce
1 small onion
¾ cup water
1 teaspoon sharp paprika
1 teaspoon chili powder
¼ teaspoon cinnamon
¼ teaspoon black pepper
1/8 teaspoon cloves

Trim all fat from the chicken, cube, and set aside. Combine all other ingredients in a large bowl, then transfer to a large skillet with high sides. Heat to medium and add the chicken cubes, simmering for 30 minutes or until cooked thoroughly. Serve with bread or 2/3 cup of brown rice.

Miso-Marinated Cod

This spicy Asian fish recipe provides plenty of healthy polyunsaturated omega-3 fatty acids, along with the rich flavors of miso and chili paste. If cod is unavailable, use any firm, flaky white fish that can be cut into thick steaks. Avoid thin species like flounder, which will not cook correctly. While the marinade itself is very salty, the practice of wrapping the fish in a porous material prevents too much salt from getting into the food itself. To make this dish ahead, simply apply the marinade, then freeze the entire dish. Defrost slowly in the refrigerator before cooking normally.

Ingredients

1 pound cod
3 tablespoons low-salt sweet white miso
1 tablespoon garlic-chili paste
2 tablespoons apple juice
2 tablespoons unprocessed cane sugar, such as turbinado

Mix together all raw ingredients except for the fish. Take a piece of plastic wrap and spread it over the counter or a cutting board, then apply a layer of miso marinade a little larger than the total surface area of the fish. Place a piece of cheesecloth on top of the marinade layer. Wrap the cheesecloth around the fish, then apply marinade to the top side. Wrap the plastic around the fish and its wrapping, then place the plastic bundle into a freezer bag. Place in the refrigerator for two hours to overnight.

Remove the fish from the refrigerator and peel away the plastic and cheesecloth layers. Heat a large nonstick frying pan over medium heat and place the fish in it. Cook on both sides until the fish is opaque and flaky throughout. Serve with low-sodium miso soup, rice and Japanese pickles. Discard any unused marinade for safety reasons.

Blackened Beef

Thinly sliced lean top round beef seared with strong spices makes for an exciting and flavorful main dish, especially when you pair it with stewed potatoes, onions and carrots. Finish the dish with tender greens for a recipe that's tasty and nutritious. This blackened beef dish is especially good with crusty low-sodium bread.

Ingredients

1 pound lean top round of beef
6 medium red potatoes
4 large onions
3 large carrots
2 cups low-sodium beef broth
2 cups water
2 cloves garlic
1 bunch kale
2 tablespoons sharp paprika
1 tablespoon dried oregano
1 teaspoon chili powder
1 teaspoon powdered garlic
½ teaspoon black pepper
¼ teaspoon red pepper
¼ teaspoon mustard powder

Place the beef in the freezer until partially frozen. Cut the potatoes into quarters, mince the garlic cloves, slice the carrots into rounds and remove the stems from the kale. Chop the onions very finely to yield about 4 cups. Combine paprika, oregano, garlic powder, chili powder, red and black peppers and dry mustard in a small bowl with a lid. Set aside. Remove beef from freezer and slice it across the grain in strips about 1/8 inch thick. Sprinkle with the seasoning mix, covering all available surfaces. Lightly grease a large heavy skillet or stockpot then preheat over high. Add the meat strips and sear, stirring continuously, for about 5 minutes.

Add the broth and water to the pan to deglaze, then add potatoes and garlic to the skillet. Allow the blackened spices to float to the top. Cover and lower heat to medium, cooking for about 20 minutes or until potatoes are tender. Add the carrots and place the kale on top of the dish. Cover and cook for an additional 10 minutes. This dish can be served right from the skillet or pot.

Feta-ricotta Greek Pizza

Many DASH dieters find that they miss conventional pizza after they start their new healthier way of eating. Getting onto the DASH diet doesn't mean you can't enjoy this classic treat, however. This whole-grain, Greek-inspired recipe provides richness with reduced fat ricotta and feta cheese, plus plenty of tasty vegetables. Adding fennel, mint and olive oil gives this recipe an authentic Mediterranean flavor. Once you learn to make these pizzas at home, you won't miss delivery.

Ingredients

10 ounces fresh or frozen spinach
3 ¼ cups low sodium marinara sauce
1 ¼ cups reduced-fat ricotta cheese
1 ¼ cups fresh mint
1 cup fresh fennel
1 whole grain 14 inch pizza crust or equivalent dough
¾ cup feta cheese crumbles
4 plum tomatoes
1 teaspoon strongly-flavored olive oil
1 teaspoon cornmeal
salt substitute and black pepper to taste

Heat a pizza stone or cookie sheet in the oven at 500

degrees Fahrenheit. Sprinkle a pizza peel with cornmeal to prevent sticking. If you are using a pizza crust, follow package instructions to prepare it for topping.

Chop the mint, tomatoes, fennel and spinach. Heat the olive oil in a large skillet to medium-high. Add the chopped fennel and sauté for five minutes, or until slightly translucent. Reduce the heat to medium-low. Drain all water from the spinach and add it to the fennel. Season with black pepper and salt substitute according to your preferences. Place the raw dough on the pizza peel and transfer it to the baking stone or sheet. Cook for 5 minutes at 500 degrees and remove from oven.

Spread the sauce over the pizza crust, then top with the spinach and fennel mixture. Spoon the ricotta in small quantities over the vegetable mixture, but do not try to spread it. Add feta crumbles and bake for another 15 minutes, or until the crust is cooked completely and the edges are lightly browned. Combine the mint and tomatoes in a separate bowl, then sprinkle them over the surface of the pizza before cutting.

Chinese Restaurant Ginger Beef

American-style Chinese food is rarely compatible with the DASH diet, but many people still miss its exciting flavors. The good news is that you can make your own at home, using far less grease, corn syrup and artificial flavors. You'll retain all the best things about restaurant Chinese dishes and avoid the sometimes sticky sauces and high glycemic index. This dish uses thinly-sliced lean beef, heart-friendly oils and fresh ginger to recreate a classic Chinese restaurant favorite.

Ingredients

¾ pound thinly-sliced flank or sirloin steak
1 medium onion
1 pound mushrooms
1 pound broccoli
2 tablespoons peanut oil
1 tablespoon rice vinegar
1 tablespoon fresh ginger
3 cloves fresh garlic
red pepper flakes to taste
salt substitute to taste

In a deep skillet or wok, heat 1 tablespoon of peanut oil on high. Mince the ginger and onion and add to the hot pan, frying for about a minute. Season with salt substitute to taste. Crush the garlic, slice the mushrooms and chop the broccoli. Add 1 teaspoon of garlic and the mushrooms to the pan. Cook for about 2 minutes, stirring throughout, or until the mushrooms soften and the onions become translucent. Add the broccoli and cook for about 3 minutes or until it is bright green and still slightly crisp. Remove the vegetables to a bowl.

Add the remaining tablespoon of peanut oil to the pan and allow it to heat. Add the beef strips and the remaining garlic, cooking for about 2 minutes. Sprinkle in the vinegar and red pepper flakes, followed by the vegetables. Stir to combine and remove from the heat immediately. Serve over short grain brown rice.

Vegetable Medley Pasta Sauce

The DASH diet works best when you reduce the amount of meat in your diet, but many people don't know where to start. This vegetable-based pasta sauce proves that you don't need to have sausage or beef to make a meal special. It uses readily-available dried herbs and fresh vegetables to provide great flavor without the meat. Serve it with your favorite whole grain pasta.

8 ounces canned low-sodium tomato sauce
6 ounces canned low-sodium tomato paste
2 medium zucchini
2 medium fresh tomatoes
2 small onions
3 cloves garlic
2 tablespoons olive oil
1 tablespoon dried oregano
1 tablespoon dried basil
1 teaspoon dried rosemary
1 cup water

Heat the olive oil in a medium-sized skillet. Mince the garlic and onions. Chop the zucchini and tomatoes coarsely. Add all vegetables to the pan and sauté for about 5 minutes over medium-high heat, or until the onions become slightly translucent. Mix the tomato paste and water in a medium bowl until smooth. Add to the pan, along with the tomato sauce and herbs. Cover and reduce the heat to low. Simmer for 45 minutes or until the sauce reaches the desired consistency. Season with salt substitute if desired.

Portabella Mushroom "Burgers"

Not every sandwich you eat on a bun has to be a hamburger. These grilled or pan-seared Portobello mushrooms are marinated in a tasty mixture of vinegar, garlic, cayenne and olive oil, leaving them anything but bland. When you accompany them with the traditional burger toppings, they make the perfect addition to any picnic, potluck or outdoor grilling occasion. Unlike a conventional hamburger, these sandwiches are low in calories, contain almost no fat, and are cholesterol-free.

Ingredients

4 large portabella mushrooms
5 tablespoons balsamic vinegar
2 tablespoons strongly-flavored olive oil
1 tablespoon raw sugar
1 clove garlic
¼ teaspoon sharp paprika

Wash the mushrooms and remove their stems. Place the mushroom caps in an oven-safe glass dish, stem side up. Mince the garlic and combine it with the olive oil, paprika, sugar and vinegar in a separate small bowl. Drizzle this mixture over the mushrooms. Cover and place in the refrigerator for ½ hour. Flip the mushrooms and marinate for an additional ½ hour.

Preheat the broiler or an outdoor grill to moderate heat. If cooking on a grill, lightly coat the rack with cooking spray. Grill or broil the mushrooms on a rack about 6 inches away from the flame, turning periodically and basting with marinade. Transfer to a plate and allow to rest for a few minutes before serving on whole grain buns with lettuce, tomato, onion and low-sodium pickles.

Sides

Baked Macaroni and Cheese

Macaroni and cheese are classic, hearty and comforting, but traditional recipes rely on butter, cream and very large amounts of full fat cheese. The result may be delightful to the taste buds, but it's hard on your arteries. Consider this version instead, which adds ripe tomatoes and reduced fat dairy to produce a baked dish that's delicious without harming your heart. Eat it as a side to an ordinary dinner or with a salad as a light meal all by itself.

Ingredients

2 cups whole grain macaroni
2 cups skim milk
8 ounces reduced fat cheddar cheese
2 fresh tomatoes
2 tablespoons margarine
1 tablespoon flour
1 small onion
1 teaspoon parsley
¼ teaspoon mustard powder
¼ teaspoon black pepper

Grate the cheese and slice the tomatoes and onion very thinly. Boil the macaroni in water according to package instructions, until al dente. Preheat the oven to 400 degrees Fahrenheit and melt margarine over medium-high heat in a sauce pan. Add mustard, flour, pepper and onion, sautéing until the onion becomes translucent. Stir in the milk slowly and cook until smooth and thickened. Add the cheese and stir until just melted. Drain the macaroni and transfer it to a 2 quart baking dish. Pour the cheese mixture over the macaroni and toss gently. Arrange the tomato slices on top of the dish and sprinkle with parsley. Bake for 20 minutes or until the top browns slightly.

Spicy Steamed Eggplant with Peanut Sauce

While most eggplant dishes are best served warm, this unusual side is an excellent cold option for summer. Preparation is quick and easy, and the finished recipe plates up attractively. Make this Asian-inspired dish on hot summer evenings when you don't feel like cooking. Look for long, thin purple Chinese eggplants and serve with cold noodles or rice.

Ingredients

1 ½ pounds eggplant, preferably Asian varieties
2 tablespoons crunchy peanut butter
1 ½ tablespoons low-sodium soy sauce
1 tablespoon apple juice
½ teaspoon chili paste
1 bunch parsley for garnish

Peel the eggplants using a small knife or vegetable peeler, removing the stem from each one. Wrap each eggplant loosely in damp cheesecloth or paper towels and arrange them in a circle around a microwave-safe plate or vegetable steamer. To prepare in the microwave, cook on the high setting for 5 minutes, turning once halfway through cooking. To prepare on the stovetop, steam in a large pot until the eggplant is soft and slightly translucent. Remove the hot eggplants from the microwave or pan and drop them immediately into a bowl of cold water. Remove the cheesecloth or paper towels and cut the vegetables on the diagonal into slices. Arrange on a plate with parsley and chill in the refrigerator.

For the sauce, combine all other ingredients in a small saucepan. Cook, stirring continuously, over medium-low heat until the peanut butter melts and all ingredients are well combined. Spoon over the chilled eggplant and serve.

Braised Spring Vegetables

This hearty combination of winter and new spring vegetables is a great choice when the weather is just beginning to warm. Serve it alongside your favorite meat as a side dish, or eat it on its own as a light lunch or a snack. This recipe is delicious both hot and cold!

Ingredients

1 pound small red, yellow or purple potatoes
1 large carrot
1 medium onion
1 cup green peas, fresh or frozen
½ pound green beans, fresh or frozen
1 clove garlic
½ tablespoon low-sodium soy sauce
1 teaspoon olive oil

Wash all the vegetables and cut the potatoes, carrot and onion into bite size pieces. Top, tail and snap the green beans if you are using fresh vegetables. Mince the garlic. Heat the olive oil in the bottom of a heavy skillet or pan over medium-low heat. Add the potatoes and cook for about 10 minutes or until they begin to brown, stirring occasionally. Add the carrots and cook for another 10 minutes, until both vegetables have begun to tenderize.

Add the sliced onions and garlic. Cook until they become transparent. Fill the pan with water to cover the potatoes and add the green vegetables. Cook until the beans and peas are bright green and tender, but not mushy. Season with soy sauce at the very end of the cooking process.

Rice Pilaf with Saffron

This rice dish is inspired by South Asian pilau, which often include fruit and nuts. Any brown rice will provide the nutty flavor and fiber that are ideal in this recipe, but the best choice is a very dark brown, strong-tasting rice that will provide an appealing contrast for the apricots. Serve this dish hot, as a side for curries or kebabs. If saffron is not available, you can substitute safflower or turmeric for a slightly different flavor.

2 ¼ cups vegetable stock
1 ¼ cups long grain brown rice
¼ cup pistachios
¼ cup dried apricots
3 tablespoons orange juice
1 ½ tablespoons canola, coconut or sunflower oil
¼ teaspoon saffron
salt substitute to taste

Combine the rice, stock and saffron in a medium saucepan. Bring to a boil over high heat. Reduce the heat to low and cover, simmering until the rice has become tender and absorbed all the liquid. Transfer to a large bowl. Combine the orange juice, oil and salt substitute in a small bowl. Pour this mixture over the rice. Chop the apricots. Heat a small skillet to medium and add the fruit and nuts, stirring continuously until the pistachios brown slightly and develop an oily appearance. Toss the fruit and nuts with the flavored rice to mix. Serve right away.

Spicy Garlic Green Beans

Green beans are a classic side dish for all kinds of cuisines, but too many people boil out the nutrients or serve them with copious amounts of butter. Instead of weighing down your beans, celebrate their crisp flavor with this spicy but appealing recipe. Blanching helps set the color and ensures an attractive dish, while a quick sauté with strongly-flavored
ingredients keeps the beans from blending into the background.

Ingredients

1 pound fresh, raw green beans
1 sweet red bell pepper
2 cloves garlic
2 teaspoons extra virgin olive oil
1 teaspoon dark sesame oil
½ teaspoon salt substitute
½ teaspoon chili paste
¼ teaspoon black pepper

Top and tail the beans, removing any strings, and snap them into 2 inch pieces. Bring a large pan of water to a boil over high heat and add the snapped beans. Cook for about 3 minutes, until they become bright green and crisp-tender. Remove the beans from the water and plunge them immediately into a bowl of ice water. Drain and place in a large bowl.

Remove the stem, ribs and seeds from the red bell pepper and cut it into thin strips about 2 inches in length. Heat the olive oil in a large frying pan over medium heat. Add the pepper, stir-frying for about a minute. Add the beans and cook for and additional minute. Crush the garlic and combine with the chili paste, salts substitute and pepper in a small bowl. Add this mixture to the vegetables, stirring to coat. Serve drizzled with sesame oil.

Salads

Spicy Tuna Salad

While the DASH diet emphasizes healthy foods that are lower in fat and cholesterol, that doesn't mean you can't enjoy your favorites. This tuna salad recipe relies on flavorful tomatoes, onions, limes and jalapenos, allowing you to reduce the sodium and cholesterol in other ingredients without losing out on taste.

Ingredients

12 oz. low sodium tuna (about 2 cans)
1/8 cup olive oil or low-fat mayonnaise
1 jalapeno pepper
1 tomato
1 small sweet onion
1 small lime

Drain the water from the tuna and place it in a medium bowl with the mayonnaise. Remove the stem, seeds and ribs from the pepper, dicing it finely. Dice the tomato and the onion. Add the vegetables and lime juice to the bowl and mix thoroughly. Serve with DASH-friendly crackers or bread.

Tabbouleh with Tomatoes

Tabbouleh is a mint-flavored cold salad popular in northern Africa and Western Asia. When made with whole grains, it provides plenty of nutritious fiber, along with refreshing vegetables. The tart flavor of this salad can take a little time to get used to, but it's an extremely welcome change when hot weather comes along. Serve tabbouleh on its own or as a side with kebabs or barbecued meats and vegetables.

Ingredients

½ pound whole grain bulgur wheat
½ pound cucumbers
½ pound fresh tomatoes
3 medium red onions
2 cups flat leaf parsley
½ cup fresh mint
3 lemons
1 tablespoon olive oil
½ teaspoon black pepper

Place the wheat in a large bowl and cover it with water. Soak for one hour or longer, until the grain has absorbed water and plumped. Chop all the vegetables into small cubes or dice and set aside. Drain the bulgur and mix it with the vegetables. Juice the lemons, removing the seeds but reserving the pulp. Add the lemon juice, herbs, oil and pepper to the mixture. Place it in a covered bowl and refrigerate for one to 12 hours. This salad can be stored as is for several days or up to a week with the onions omitted.

Edamame Salad

Fresh, steamed soybeans are known as Edamame in Japan, and are eaten as an appetizer or part of other dishes. When served cold, these beans also make a great salad ingredient. This recipe combines them with cherry tomatoes, fresh mint, dill and scallions. A light oil and vinegar dressing finishes it for a fresh-tasting start to any meal. Try it with a little feta or other salty cheese for added contrast.

Ingredients

½ pound fresh Edamame
1 pint cherry or grape tomatoes
¼ cup red wine vinegar
1 ½ tablespoons extra virgin olive oil
1 scallion
1 small bunch fresh dill weed
1 small bunch fresh mint
¼ teaspoon black pepper

Place the soybeans in a steamer over about an inch of water. Cover and steam for approximately 5 minutes, or until the pods are bright green and the beans are crisp-tender. Rinse with cold water and remove from the pods. Set the beans aside in a medium bowl and refrigerate. Chop the mint and dill finely. Slice the green onion. Cut large cherry tomatoes into halves, leaving small ones whole. Combine tomatoes, green onion, mint and dill in a medium bowl. Mix oil, vinegar and black pepper in a small bowl and pour over the salad. Serve chilled.

Raw Okra Salad

Many people associate okra with slimy boiled preparations or greasy fried food. This unusual member of the mallow family doesn't have to be cooked, however. When sliced carefully and served raw, it has an exciting crispness and lacks any unappealing mucilage. Combine it with spicy mixed salad greens, jicama and sweet peppers for a refreshing salad that's a little outside the usual fare.

Ingredients

1 cup fresh okra
1/3 pound fresh salad greens
1 pound jicama
1 small sweet red bell pepper
4 tablespoons low sodium poppy-seed salad dressing
¼ teaspoon salt substitute
1/4 teaspoon black pepper

Remove the stems from the okra and slice them in half vertically, using a clean, absolutely dry knife. Wipe the knife off between pieces to reduce mucilage production. Remove the stem, seeds and ribs from the pepper and cut it into strips. Peel and slice the jicama into matchsticks. Combine the okra, salad greens, pepper and jicama in a large bowl. Toss gently and season with salt substitute and fresh pepper. Top with poppy-seed dressing and serve immediately.

Tomato-Zucchini Salad with Eggs

Squash and tomatoes are abundant and at their best in the heat of summer, which is the best time to make this refreshing salad. The addition of eggs provides a little more heartiness and allows this dish to act as a light lunch or a starter. For a slightly different flavor, consider using different types of fresh herbs.

Ingredients

2 pounds zucchini
2 pounds ripe tomatoes
6 to 8 eggs
½ cup fresh basil
Dressing:
2 tablespoons extra virgin olive oil
¼ cup red wine vinegar
1 tablespoon fresh parsley
1 teaspoon raw sugar

Combine all dressing ingredients in a glass bowl and mix thoroughly. Set aside. Slice the zucchini and tomatoes into thin rounds. Bring one large and one small pot of water to a boil. Place the eggs in one pot, immediately cover, and reduce heat. Plunge the zucchini rounds into the larger pot for 2 to 3 minutes. Remove from the pot and place immediately in ice water. Drain completely and arrange alternately with the tomato slices on a large plate. Drain the eggs and place them in a bowl of ice water. Peel and slice, arranging the slices on top of the zucchini and tomato rounds. Cover with basil leaves, then drizzle vinegar mixture over the entire platter.

Low Cholesterol Potato Salad

Traditional potato salad is a must at many picnics, but it's loaded with cholesterol, fat and sodium. All of these ingredients can be hazardous for your heart, so many DASH dieters feel as though potato salad is off the menu. This recipe offers much of the same creamy taste and texture, but without the fat and salt. Bring it to your next picnic and no one will ever worry about it being "health food."

Ingredients

1 pound yellow or red waxy potatoes
1 large yellow sweet onion
2 stalks celery
1 large carrot
¼ cup reduced-calorie mayonnaise
2 tablespoons dill weed
2 tablespoons red wine vinegar
1 tablespoon prepared brown mustard

Boil the potatoes in their skins, allow to cool, and dice. Mince the onion and dill weed. Dice the carrot and celery into small pieces. Combine the mayonnaise, mustard, vinegar, pepper and dill in a large bowl. Stir in the vegetables, mixing to coat the pieces completely.

Cover and refrigerate for one hour to overnight to allow the flavors to mingle. Serve chilled.

Soups

Nutrient-packed Kale Soup

The unique, slightly-nutty taste of kale makes this soup an interesting and satisfying starter for any cold season meal, while providing a wide range of healthy vitamins. Adding homemade croutons gives this creamy recipe a hearty crunch without too much fat or too many processed carbohydrates. Plus, their freshness will help them outshine any store-bought option. Enjoy this soup whenever the weather turns chilly and kale is readily available.

Ingredients

6 cups fresh kale leaves
4 cups low sodium broth or stock, preferably vegetable
3 medium red potatoes
1 small white onion
1 tablespoon olive oil
1 tablespoon fresh thyme
1 clove fresh garlic
½ teaspoon black pepper
¼ teaspoon salt substitute
Croutons:

2 cups day old whole grain bread pieces
2 tablespoons olive oil
1 tablespoon fresh thyme
1 tablespoon fresh parsley
1 teaspoon garlic powder

Trim the kale leaves and remove any tough ribs. Chop the onion and the potatoes into small dice. Crush the garlic. Heat 1 tablespoon of olive oil in a heavy pan over medium heat and sauté the chopped onion, crushed garlic and fresh thyme for 7 to 8 minutes or until the onions are transparent. Add the diced potatoes, salt substitute and pepper. Stir well and cook for another 10 minutes or until the potatoes have begun to soften. Remove the cover and add the kale. Cook uncovered for 5 minutes, then add broth, cover and heat for an additional 5 minutes or until the kale becomes bright green and tender. Place half of the soup in a food processor or blender and process until completely smooth. Return this mixture to the saucepan and mix thoroughly.

Croutons: Cut or break bread into pieces approximately ½ inch across. Combine garlic powder, 2 tablespoons olive oil and herbs in a large bowl and add the bread. Toss to coat the outside of the bread but do not allow the oil to soak in. Place croutons on a baking sheet lined with foil and bake at 350 degrees for about 10 minutes or until the outsides are crisp and golden. Cool and use to top bowls of hot soup.

Meatless Lentil Chili

This tasty vegetarian alternative to conventional chili is hearty and flavorful, with bulgur wheat and lentils replacing the usual fatty beef and chili beans. If you're trying to reduce the number of days on which you eat meat, this chili is a great way to start. Serve with diced scallions, low fat sour cream or a DASH-friendly cornbread. For a more interesting chili, substitute red, yellow or black lentils for the traditional brown variety.

Ingredients

3 cups low-sodium vegetable broth
2 cups or one can chopped tomatoes
1 cup bulgur wheat
1 cup dried lentils
1 medium white onion
4 cloves garlic
2 tablespoons canola oil
2 ½ tablespoons chili powder
1 tablespoon cumin powder
½ teaspoon cinnamon
Salt substitute and pepper to taste

Heat the oil to medium-high in a large pot. Mince the onion and garlic, then add them to the pot and cook for

5 minutes, stirring continuously. When the alliums have become slightly translucent, add the wheat and lentils, followed by the broth. Stir to combine, then add the tomatoes and spices. Bring to a boil over high heat, then reduce to low and cover. Simmer for 30 minutes or until the lentils just begin to fall apart. Add salt substitute and pepper to taste and serve hot.

Tangy Carrot Curry

This smooth soup contains plenty of exciting spices, along with protein-rich low fat yogurt and bright, tangy cilantro. The result is an antioxidant-filled dish you'll enjoy with a fresh salad and a slice of homestyle whole-grain bread. For a spicier version, substitute cayenne or Thai peppers for the jalapeno.

Ingredients

5 cups low-sodium vegetable stock
1 pound carrots
1 large yellow onion
1 jalapeno pepper
¼ cup cilantro leaves
¼ cup low fat unsweetened yogurt
2 tablespoons lime or lemon juice
1 tablespoon sunflower oil
1 tablespoon fresh ginger
2 cloves garlic
2 teaspoons Madras curry powder
1 teaspoon black mustard seeds
salt substitute to taste

Heat the olive oil in a large saucepan to medium. Mince the garlic and ginger and chop the onion finely. Add the mustard seed to the oil and allow it to pop, then add the ginger, garlic and onion. Cook for about 5 minutes, stirring continuously, or until the onions become translucent but not brown. Remove the stem, seeds and ribs of the jalapeno and chop it finely, then add to the pan along with the curry powder. Chop the carrots roughly and sauté with the other ingredients for about 3 minutes, or until the seasonings begin to toast. Pour in about half of the stock and bring the whole pot to a boil over high heat. Reduce to medium-low and simmer for about 5 minutes, or until the carrots become tender.

Remove the soup from the pot and place it in a blender or food processor. Process until the liquid is smooth, in batches if necessary, and return to the pan. Stir in the remaining stock and reheat. Add yogurt, cilantro and lime juice, as well as salt substitute to taste. Garnish with additional cilantro and limes before serving.

Cream of Wild Rice Soup with Fennel

Traditional cream of rice soups are extremely comforting, but they're also heavy on butter, cream and refined carbohydrates, making them unsuitable for the DASH diet. Instead, consider this version. It gets its creaminess from white beans and low fat milk and includes vitamin-packed kale and carrots. If wild rice is unavailable in your area, consider substituting any long grain brown rice, such as Basmati, or red rice.

2 cups 1 percent or skim milk
2 cups low-sodium vegetable stock
1 ½ cups kale
1 cup cooked white beans, unsalted
¼ cup wild rice
2 stalks celery
1 large sweet onion
1 large carrot
1 tablespoon fresh parsley
½ tablespoon vegetable oil
1 teaspoon fennel
1 teaspoon black pepper
salt substitute to taste

Place wild rice in a small pot and cover with water. Bring to a boil over high heat, then reduce heat and simmer until the rice has become tender but chewy, or about one hour. Dice the carrot, celery, onion and parsley. Heat the vegetable oil in a large pot over medium heat, then add the onion, carrot, celery and spices. Cook, stirring periodically, until the onions are translucent, the carrots have become slightly tender. Add the parsley, kale and stock. Season with salt substitute to taste.

Combine the milk with the cooked white beans in a blender or food processor. Puree until smooth and add gradually to the soup, stirring continuously. Bring to a simmer and add the cooked rice. Simmer for an additional 30 minutes or until flavors have diffused. Serve with crusty low-sodium bread.

Hearty Turkey Soup

This recipe isn't just a way to use up the leftovers from a big holiday meal, it's also a hearty low-sodium option that includes plenty of healthy winter vegetables. Serve big bowls of this dish with rice or bread as meals on their own, or as a side for lunch or dinner.

Ingredients

Carcass from one turkey
2 quarts low-sodium chicken or vegetable broth
1 quart water
4 large yellow onions
1 large turnip
1 pound carrots
2 cups tomatoes, fresh or canned
2 cups cooked white beans, home-cooked or canned
½ pound light turkey
¼ cup hulled whole barley
1/3 cup fresh parsley
½ teaspoon black pepper
¼ teaspoon thyme
1 bay leaf
salt substitute to taste

Place the turkey carcass in a large stockpot with the

broth and water. Bring to a boil over high heat. Chop one onion into quarters and add to the pot. Reduce the heat, cover, and allow the pot to simmer for an hour. Remove all solids from the pot and place the stock in the refrigerator for 2 hours to overnight. Skim off any fat from the cooled broth and discard. Return the broth to its original pot.

Chop the carrots, turnip, tomatoes and remaining onions and add them to the broth. Add the bay leaf, beans, barley, herbs and spices to the mixture, stirring to combine. Cut the turkey meat into bite-sized chunks and add to the pot. Bring the entire mixture to a simmer, then cover and allow to cook for an hour or until all the vegetables have softened. Serve immediately.

DASH Diet 5-Day Sample Menu

Deciding how to eat on the DASH diet plan can be tricky if you're not used to dealing with its rules. Here's a quick 5-day sample menu using some recipes from this book to help you get started. There's no reason to stick to just this menu, however. You can mix and match the recipes or use foods of your own. Just make sure that you stick to the guidelines set forth earlier in this book and it'll be hard to go wrong!

Day 1

Breakfast: Fresh orange juice, whole grain toast with low-sugar fruit spread, DASH-Friendly Oatmeal

Lunch: Tangy Carrot Curry, fresh vegetable crudités, brown rice
Snack: almonds, hazelnuts or cashews, fresh peach or nectarine

Dinner: Blackened Beef, Tabbouleh with Tomatoes, Chewy Fruit Bars

Day 2

Breakfast: Healthy Homemade Granola, fresh strawberries, skim milk

Lunch: Miso-Marinated Cod, Edamame Salad, hot green tea

Snack: fat-free, low-sugar yogurt, graham crackers

Dinner: Chinese Restaurant Ginger Beef, brown rice, fresh oranges

Day 3

Breakfast: Toasted Breakfast Sandwich, fresh orange juice

Lunch: Spicy Tuna Salad on whole grain bread with lettuce and tomato,
Sugar Free Agua Fresca

Snack: Pretzels, raisins, sunflower seeds

Dinner: Feta-ricotta Greek Pizza, lettuce hearts, olives

Day 4

Breakfast: Peanut Butter and Banana Smoothie, whole grain bagel with light cream cheese

Lunch: Meatless lentil chili, low-sodium cornbread, tomatoes, low-fat sour cream

Snack: Vegetable Sushi

Dinner: Simple Grilled Chicken, Braised Spring Vegetables, vanilla wafers

Day 5

Breakfast: Chewy Fruit Bars, Spicy, Sweet and Tangy Herbal Tea

Lunch: Tomato-Zucchini Salad with Eggs, whole grain pasta with
Vegetable Medley Pasta Sauce

Snack: apple, whole grain crackers

Dinner: Portabella Mushroom "Burgers", Low Cholesterol Potato Salad, low fat frozen yogurt

Modifying the 5-Day Meal Plan

Because every person has different calorie requirements, it's hard to say how much you'll need to eat of these foods at any given meal. If you take a little time to look at your activity level and personal habits, you'll have an easier time choosing the right calorie level for you. The main DASH diet offers 1,200, 1,600, 2,000 and 2,400 calorie options for various amounts of activity and various metabolisms. In general, if you're hoping to lose weight, consider choosing a calorie goal that's one rung lower than the one you need to maintain.

That means that if you're relatively active but overweight, you could move down from the 2,000 calories that you probably need to stay at your current weight, choosing a 1,600 calorie per day diet, instead. You'd aim to get the same 4 to 5 servings of fruits and vegetables per day, as well as the same 3 to 4 servings of low fat dairy, nuts and beans, but you'd limit your meat consumption to just 5 ounces per day and cut back on fats and sweets. It may take a little while to figure things out, but you can help it along by doubling up on low calorie vegetables, fruits and non-fat dairy while limiting meat, cheese and grain consumption.

Conclusion

The average American diet is high in unhealthy fried food and high-fat meat and dairy sources, as well as too much sugar. The result, for many people, is skyrocketing blood pressure and an increased risk of heart disease and stroke. If you're worried that your health could be at risk, it's time to take steps.

That means moving to the DASH diet and avoiding unhealthy foods in favor of rich, flavorful options that are low in fat and high in vitamins. While it's true that the adjustment period may take a little longer than you expect, all these recipes will help you make the transition. You won't miss the fat or extra sugar! Just focus on the healthy foods that you can eat and work to make fruits and vegetables a regular part of your routine. Your heart and your waistline will thank you.

Section 2: Grain Free Cooking

Grain free eating can be hard to think about in a culture that uses flour, corn and other refined starches in almost every food. For some of us, however, grains aren't the healthiest option. Mounting evidence suggests that heavy carbohydrate consumption simply isn't ideal for a significant portion of the population. If you're among these people, you're better off choosing a protein-heavy diet that helps you keep your blood sugar consistent and reduces your risk of diabetes and similar conditions.

For others, the gluten found in a wide variety of grains like wheat, rye and some oats can cause serious digestive and metabolic problems. Whether you have a grain allergy or you suffer from gluten intolerances such as celiac disease, your body simply can't digest grains properly. In severe cases, the nutritional deficiencies caused by this problem can lead to fuzzy thinking, deterioration of the bones and teeth, and even serious mood disorders. The solution is simple: just discontinue grains.

Last but not least, you may wish to avoid grains if you're following a paleo-style diet. These eating plans focus on the foods that were available to our ancestors before the advent of agriculture. That means that grains were consumed infrequently at best, and they were never processed into flour or other highly refined products. The diet relies much more heavily on fresh fruits, vegetables, tubers and animal products such as meat. If you follow a paleo diet, you'll find plenty of material here to keep your taste buds happy and your body healthy.

The Problem of Grains

Grains such as wheat, rice, corn, barley and rye have been an essential part of human diets all over the world since the invention of agriculture. They are appealing, easy to produce in large quantities, and simple to cook. Unfortunately, they aren't necessarily the ideal option for many people. Modern varieties of grains may be especially prone to problems. They have been modified extensively from their ancestral form, containing far more starch and less fiber than their ancestors. In many cases, they seem to be more likely to cause metabolic diseases, intolerances and other problems than even the grains that were available just a century ago.

The problem becomes even more serious when genetically-modified foods appear on the scene. While the basic mechanism of genetic modification is the same whether the process occurs in the field through breeding or in a lab, modern science makes gene tinkering extremely easy. We don't know whether this process has any significant side effects, however. Since many of the grains currently on the market have been genetically modified, it can be hard to tell whether they're having an effect on your health.

These issues are part of why so many people are choosing to limit or eliminate grains in their diet. While grain free dieting isn't for everyone, a significant percentage of the people who try it find themselves feeling stronger, more energetic and healthier. Headaches, excess weight gain and even some long-lasting health problems decrease and even vanish in many people. In many cases, it seems as though our bodies simply aren't meant to use grains in the forms that are currently available.

Transitioning to a Grain Free Diet

If you have reason to believe that you could benefit from a grain free diet, you may still have trouble making the leap. After all, most cultures still have a basic diet that is built on one or more grains. Whether it's the ubiquitous bread found in North American and European cooking, the corn we see in so much native and Central American cuisine, or the rice found throughout Asia, grains seem to be everywhere. By choosing to eliminate them from your diet, you have to deliberately go against the flow. Many people who are seeking to cut out excess grain consumption have run into trouble finding good, healthy recipes to help them.

The key is to approach the process carefully and with a well-defined plan. If you're hoping to cut your carbohydrates or want to use a paleo-inspired diet plan, you may want to slowly substitute more grain free foods in your diet. Over time, you can replace your favorites with foods that are just as delicious, without seriously disrupting your life.

For others this method won't work as well. This is the case if you know you have a serious allergy or intolerance to one or more grains. You may also have trouble with the slow substitution technique if you are using specific kinds of low carbohydrate diets. In these cases, you'll need to start over from scratch. Remove all the grain based foods from your home and avoid picking up new ones to reduce temptation.

No matter how you make the transition, it's important to have a plan. Haphazardly trying to start on a new way of eating is one of the surest ways to guarantee the failure of this lifestyle change. Instead, make sure you have a good idea of what's available to you in your new, grain-free lifestyle, and choose the most appealing foods you possibly can. It's much easier to make the switch when you know that you have something to look forward to.

A Question of Nutritional Balance

If you're like many people, you're probably used to getting the bulk of your nutrition from grain-based foods such as bread or pasta. That can make transitioning to a diet that's lower in or completely free of grains a little daunting. After all, no one wants to discover that they've been eating a nutritionally imbalanced diet after making this kind of change, and many government health organizations recommend eating up to 11 servings of grains every day.

In reality, consuming this many grain-based products isn't necessary for good health. Many cultures consume far less, basing their diets on non-grain starches, fresh fruits and vegetables, and healthy meats with no significant health issues. As long as you pay attention to the basic recommendations of your specific grain-free diet plan or your nutritionist, you shouldn't have too many problems with balance. Focus on eating a variety of different foods instead of just the same few every day, and you'll soon be feeling healthier and happier than you ever did while consuming lots of processed grains.

Grain Free Shopping and Cooking Tips

Shopping for grain-free foods can be extremely difficult, especially if you're used to consuming a lot of convenience foods. That's because many apparently non-grain products actually contain extremely processed grain ingredients. For instance, many ketchups, pasta sauces and even commercial French fries have been treated with dextrose, glucose and maltodextrin. These sweeteners are derived from corn or rice, and they can be incompatible with a non-grain diet.

You may also find grains in non-dairy milks, baking powder, spice mixes, flavored beverages and many other foods. If you choose any kind of prepared meat, such as pre-made hamburger patties, there is a good chance that a corn, wheat, or rice-based thickener and binder has been used in its preparation. Even soy sauce usually contains hidden wheat unless otherwise labeled. Read packages carefully and avoid any product that contains thickeners, malt ingredients, dextrose and similar sweeteners, non-specific starches such as modified food starch, or ingredients labeled simply as "vegetable" or "plant" proteins.

It's also important to be careful in the kitchen, especially if you suffer from an allergy or intolerance. In shared cooking spaces, it's very easy for grains from a roommate or family member's cooking to end up in your food. Wash all knives, cutting boards, counters and containers carefully before using them to reduce the risk of contamination. While this may not be a concern for everyone, in some cases even a small amount of a grain-based product can make you very sick.

Reading the Recipe Key

Since there are so many reasons to seek out grain free recipes, not every meal will be right for every kind of diet. This book uses the symbols **GF**, **P** and **LC** to mark gluten-free, paleo and low carbohydrate recipes to ensure that you can quickly and easily find the perfect dish for your next meal. While most recipes will meet the requirements of more than one type of diet, it's important to check before you start cooking if you want to ensure perfect nutrition for your dietary requirements.

Breakfast

No-Grain Granola (GF, P, LC)

Breakfast cereal is an important part of many people's regular daily routine, but it can be hard to have cereal without grains. This no-grain granola recipe relies on fresh raw nuts and seeds rather than oats or wheat. It's sweetened naturally with dates and uses no oil, so it's suitable for all kinds of low-carbohydrate diets. You'll enjoy this rich, delicious and very natural breakfast option, whether you have it with fresh fruit and your favorite dairy or plant milk or you eat it on its own. To increase the sweetness, just add more date paste.

Ingredients

2 cups raw pecans
2 cups raw cashews or Brazil nuts
2 cups raw pumpkin or sunflower seeds
1 cup plain coconut flakes
1 cup dates
1 cup water
½ cup flax seeds
1 vanilla bean or 2 teaspoons vanilla extract

½ teaspoon cinnamon or mixed sweet spices

Place the whole nuts and seeds in a large bowl and cover them with lukewarm water, stirring to combine. Allow to rest at room temperature for 8 hours to 2 days. This process sprouts the seeds and removes phytic acid, which can cause digestive problems. In a food processor or blender, combine the dates and 1 cup of warm to hot water. Process for about 1 minute, or until a smooth paste is formed. Split the vanilla bean and scrape out the contents.

Drain the nuts and seeds, then add the coconut flakes, flax seeds, vanilla, date paste, vanilla scrapings and cinnamon. Stir to combine. Line a baking sheet with parchment paper and pour the granola mixture out onto it, spreading into an even layer. Dehydrate in 170 degree Fahrenheit oven for about 8 hours or until the granola is crunchy. Stir periodically to break up clumps. Allow to cool and place in an airtight container for storage. This mixture lasts for 3 to 4 weeks at room temperature.

Fresh Homestyle Beef Sausages (GF, P, LC)

Most commercial sausage recipes rely on grains as fillers and binders for the meat. This makes the sausage easier to prepare and protects the manufacturer's bottom line, but it can be disaster for your grain-free diet. Making your own sausage at home is a surprisingly simple way to enjoy this classic breakfast meat without worrying about the inclusion of oatmeal, wheat, pork or other undesirable substances. For a different flavor, substitute chicken.

Ingredients

2 pounds grass-fed boneless chuck steak
1 tablespoon fresh thyme
1 tablespoon fresh sage
¾ tablespoon coarse salt
½ teaspoon red pepper or sharp paprika

Trim the fat from the meat and discard, then chop the beef into cubes approximately 1 inch across. Freeze on a baking sheet for about 20 minutes, or until the texture is relatively firm. Combine the herbs, pepper or paprika and salt in a small bowl. Remove the meat from the freezer. Place ½ of it in the refrigerator and place the other half in the bowl of a powerful food processor.

Sprinkle with about ½ of the spice mixture and pulse until the meat is in very small pieces and the spices are well incorporated throughout.

Spread a piece of parchment paper on a counter or cutting board and transfer the meat to the center of the paper. Roll the paper around the meat to form a log, twisting the ends to secure them or using a rubber band. Repeat the process with the remaining meat and spices to form two fat sausages. Freeze for 30 minutes before cooking to make the slicing process easier. Cook in ¼ inch thick slices over medium-high heat and serve with eggs, sauces, soup or on pizzas. This recipe can be frozen for up to 2 months without loss of flavor.

Almond Cottage Cheese Pancakes (GF, P*, LC**)

Pancakes and other breakfast sweets can be hard to come by when you're on a grain-free diet, but that doesn't mean you have to give them up completely. This recipe uses starches derived from tubers, not grains, along with flour from nuts and seeds. If you've been missing that classic pancake breakfast, this is the recipe for you.

Ingredients

½ cup almond flour
½ cup cottage cheese
3 large eggs
1/8 cup coconut flour
1 tablespoon raw honey
3/8 teaspoon baking powder
¼ teaspoon cream of tartar or lemon juice
¼ teaspoon plain gelatin granules
¼ teaspoon vanilla extract
salt to taste
2 tablespoons coconut oil

Place the almond flour, cottage cheese, eggs, coconut flour, honey, baking powder, cream of tartar, gelatin, vanilla and salt in a food processor or blender and process until combined and completely smooth. Heat 1 tablespoon of coconut oil in a heavy-bottomed skillet or griddle to medium-high. Spoon the batter into the pan in a thin layer about 4 inches across and cook until the bottom is golden and the top looks relatively dry. Flip and cook until the other side has browned. Remove the cakes from the pan and repeat until all batter has been consumed. Serve with fruit, yogurt, honey, syrup or jam.

*This recipe is not suitable for paleo dieters who avoid dairy products or eggs.

** To make this recipe low-carbohydrate friendly, omit the honey or substitute a no-calorie liquid sweetener according to package instructions.

Open-faced Apple, Egg and Salmon Sandwich (GF, P, LC)

This breakfast recipe combines the richness of egg with the sharp sweetness of a tart baking apple and the salty savor of salmon. Look for organic apples whenever possible. This recipe makes four sandwiches, but it's easy to cut back to serve just one or two.

6 large eggs
4 slices smoked salmon
2 large tart baking apples, such as Granny Smith
2 tablespoons coconut oil
salt and pepper to taste
Romano cheese (optional)

Crack the eggs into a medium bowl and beat until thick and creamy. Season with salt and pepper. In a medium pan, heat the coconut oil to medium-low. Pour in the eggs and allow to set, then scramble, cooking for about 5 minutes. Remove from heat. Core the apples and slice each one in half. Place the apple halves cut-side-up in an oven-safe baking dish. Top each piece of apple with a slice of salmon and ¼ of the scrambled eggs. Garnish with thinly-shaved Romano cheese if desired. Bake at 400 degrees Fahrenheit for 10 minutes, or until apples are warm throughout.

Almond Waffles (GF, P*)

Using almond flour produces a crunchy waffle that makes an excellent snack. Make sure that you preheat the waffle iron for at least 15 minutes before cooking this recipe, since a cold iron can result in trouble removing the finished waffles. Serve with fresh fruit, coconut oil or butter, cream or maple syrup.

Ingredients

2 ¾ cup almond flour
2 ¾ cups tapioca flour
2 3/4 cups water
1/4 teaspoon salt
1 tablespoon coconut oil

Brush the waffle iron with coconut oil and preheat. Combine the almond flour, tapioca flour and salt in a large bowl. Add the oil and water, stirring vigorously until well combined. Allow the batter to stand for five minutes, then remix before pouring the individual waffles. Pour about 1 ½ cups of batter into the waffle iron at a time and cook on high heat for 15 minutes or until the surface is crisp and golden. Reheat the waffle iron and re-stir the batter before cooking each set of waffles.

* Some paleo diets permit the use of starch from tubers such as tapioca or arrowroot, but this may not apply to all cases.

Green Eggs (GF, P, LC)

With or without the addition of your favorite non-pork "ham," this recipe will definitely turn heads and please your taste buds. The addition of flavorful, nutrient-dense fresh kale makes simple scrambled eggs bright green and highly unusual. For a change, consider substituting parsley or spinach instead of the kale.

Ingredients

4 large eggs
½ pound kale
coconut oil for frying
salt and black pepper to taste

Remove the ribs and stems from the kale and discard. Combine the remaining leaves with the eggs, salt and pepper in a blender and process until completely smooth. Heat the oil to high in a large skillet. Pour the egg mixture into the pan and allow it to set, then scramble gently with a silicone spatula or wooden spoon until creamy and cooked through. Serve with breakfast sausage or your favorite non-grain bread.

Hot Porridge (GF, P, LC)

Hot porridges such as oatmeal may not be romantic, but many people find that they miss these foods' simple appeal when it's time to give up grains. This comforting version is based on nuts and seeds, but it still has that creamy texture. For a savory version, substitute black pepper for the cinnamon and serve with butter, paprika, cheese or even crispy bits of turkey bacon.

Ingredients

1 cup water
¼ cup chopped walnuts
2 tablespoons plain shredded coconut
1 tablespoon pumpkin or sunflower seeds
1 tablespoon chia seeds
1 tablespoon flax seeds
1 teaspoon cinnamon
¼ teaspoon salt

Bring the water to a boil. Combine all the other ingredients in a powerful blender and process until a fine meal is produced. Pour the boiling water over the entire mixture and cover. Blend slowly, increasing the intensity, until the porridge is smooth and creamy. Serve hot, with dried fruit, cream, honey or milk.

No-Grain Breakfast Burritos (GF, P, LC)

Breakfast burritos are a tasty and convenient way to enjoy a savory start to your day. When corn and wheat tortillas are no longer an option, we turn to egg tortillas instead. Filled with taco meat, guacamole and other tasty ingredients, this also makes an excellent light lunch.

Ingredients

1 pound ground turkey
2 ripe avocados
1 small red onion
1 medium tomato
1 lime
2 cloves garlic
2 tablespoons cilantro
1 teaspoon salt
1 tablespoon grain-free taco seasoning
12 eggs
1 tablespoon grain-free hot sauce
1 tablespoon coconut oil.

In a skillet over medium heat, brown the turkey. Sprinkle the meat with 1 tablespoon of taco seasoning, stirring to combine. Remove from heat. Mash the avocados, chop the onion, tomato, cilantro and garlic, and combine in a small bowl. Season with salt and lime juice, mixing until you have achieved your preferred consistency.

In a separate skillet, heat the coconut oil to medium-low. Beat two eggs until creamy and thick. Season with salt and hot sauce, then pour a thin layer into the hot skillet. Allow to cook all the way through on one side and remove to a plate. Repeat the process until you have 12 egg tortillas. To serve, top each tortilla with a spoonful of taco meat and guacamole. Garnish with green onions or sour cream if desired.

Sweet Potato Breakfast Casserole (GF, P, LC)

This quiche-like dish uses grated sweet potatoes to produce an appealing and grain-free crust, into which are piled eggs, meat, cheese and fresh herbs. Substitute your favorites to produce variations on this exciting brunch casserole. This dish is great hot and fresh out of the oven, but it can also be served cold for lunch or a snack.

Ingredients

2 medium sweet potatoes
4 eggs
¾ cup diced turkey or your favorite breakfast sausage
2 tablespoons coconut oil
1 small onion
1 tablespoon fresh basil
1 tablespoon fresh oregano
1 tablespoon flat-leaf parsley
Salt to taste
½ cup cheddar cheese (optional)

Grate the sweet potatoes finely. Grease a pie plate using 1 teaspoon of coconut oil. Salt the sweet potatoes and press them evenly over the sides and bottom of the pan. Melt the coconut oil and pour it over the layered sweet potatoes. Bake in a 425 degree Fahrenheit oven for 20 minutes, or until crisp but not burnt. Remove and allow to cool slightly.

Spread turkey or sausage in an even layer over the bottom of the crust. Sprinkle cheese over the meat. In a small bowl, beat the eggs thoroughly. Chop the herbs and add them to the eggs. Season with salt to taste and pour over the meat and cheese. Reduce the oven temperature to 350 degrees and bake for 30 minutes or until the center is solid. Allow to set slightly, slice and serve.

Main Dishes

Pot Roast with Fresh Vegetables (GF, P, LC)

A traditional pot roast makes a great addition to almost any grain-free dinner. About half the fat in the beef is monounsaturated, or "good" fat. Plus, this meat is full of vitamin B12 and other essential nutrients. When combined with mustard, garlic and other delicious spices, it's an easy and appealing choice for just about any meal. It also freezes well, making this roast a good option for single-serving meals later.

Ingredients

5 pounds chuck roast
2 pounds mushrooms
2 large onions
1 ½ pounds carrots
4 cups butternut squash
2 cups beef broth
2 tablespoons tomato paste
2 tablespoons sunflower oil
1 small head garlic
1 tablespoon thyme

1 tablespoon sharp paprika
1 teaspoon salt
1 teaspoon black pepper
2 bay leaves

Trim the excess fat from the roast. In a small bowl, combine the salt, mustard, thyme, pepper and paprika. Rub this mixture over the outside of the roast. Heat the oil in a large Dutch oven to medium-high. Place the roast inside and brown on all sides, turning periodically. Peel and coarsely chop the onions and garlic. Add these to the pot along with the stock and tomato paste. Bring all to a simmer and cover, cooking for about 10 minutes.

Remove from heat and place the entire pot in the oven. Bake at 325 degrees Fahrenheit for 3 hours. Coarsely chop the mushrooms, carrots and squash. Remove the roast and add the vegetables, then recover and bake for an additional hour. Serve immediately right from the pot.

Tropical Tilapia (GF, P)

Once unknown, tilapia has become one of the most common whitefish options. This species has tender flesh with a mild flavor, plus it's harvested from fish that repopulate readily and live in a wide range of environments. That makes it a better choice than many traditional whitefish, whose numbers are on the decline. Originally from tropical habitats, tilapia taste delicious when combined with other hot-climate foods such as pineapple, coconut and sweet potatoes.

Ingredients

1 pound tilapia fillets
2 large sweet potatoes
1 large onion
2 cups coconut milk
1 tablespoon coconut oil
¼ cup fresh pineapple
salt and black pepper to taste

Bake, boil or steam the sweet potatoes until they are tender and remove the skins. Slice them into thick rounds. Heat a tablespoon of coconut oil in a large frying pan over medium heat. Dice the onions and cook them in the oil until they are softened and translucent, but not brown. Stir the coconut milk to emulsify any solids and add it directly to the onions. Bring to a simmer, then add the tilapia fillets in a single layer. Cook the fish in the coconut milk mixture for about 5 minutes or until the bottom side is opaque. Flip the fillets and add the pineapple in a single layer on top. Cook the entire pan for an additional five minutes, then serve on top of the sweet potato rounds. Drizzle the remaining coconut milk and onion mixture on top of the dish and season with salt and pepper.

Barbecue Chicken with Grain-free Sauce (GF, P)

Barbecue lovers are often disappointed when they go grain free, since most commercial barbecue sauce is chock full of ingredients derived from wheat, rice and corn. Fortunately, it's extremely easy to make your own delicious barbecue sauce at home. These very simple chicken wings are excellent hot or cold, and they make the perfect addition to just about any cookout.

20 chicken wings
1 cup tomato sauce
1 large juice orange
3 shallots
½ cup honey
¼ cup vinegar
2 cloves garlic
1-inch piece ginger
1 teaspoon fresh thyme
1 teaspoon salt
½ teaspoon sharp paprika

Dice the shallots, garlic and ginger finely. Combine with all ingredients other than chicken wings in a medium-sized pan and simmer over medium-low heat until the onions are soft, or about 45 minutes. Allow to cool. Wash the chicken wings and remove the tips. In a large bowl, toss the wings with ½ cup of barbecue sauce. Place them in a 9 x 13 inch casserole pan and bake at 350 degrees Fahrenheit for 30 to 45 minutes. Use the shorter time period if you intend to finish the wings on a charcoal or gas grill. Otherwise, finish by turning the oven to broil and cook for approximately 10 minutes, or until wings are properly browned. Transfer to a large bowl and toss with another ½ cup barbecue sauce, then serve.

Zucchini Pasta with Roasted Sweet Potatoes and Coconut Pesto (GF, P)

While meat makes up a big part of most grain-free diets, that doesn't mean it has to appear in every meal. This pasta-style squash dish is light and delicious, with a rich pesto-based sauce and plenty of protein from coconut. It also includes sweet potatoes to help ensure that it's filling as well as tasty. Unlike many of the recipes in this book, this zucchini pasta is best eaten fresh and does not store well.

Ingredients

2 large zucchinis
2 medium sweet potatoes
1 cup mixed greens
1 cup fresh basil
½ cup plain shredded coconut
½ cup hot water
¼ cup olive oil
1 lemon
salt and black pepper to taste

Cut the zucchini into long ribbons using a spiral slicer or a paring knife. Chop the sweet potatoes into large pieces and toss with 1 tablespoon olive oil. Place in an oven-safe dish and roast at 375 degrees until tender. Set aside and allow to cool. Bring a pot of water to a boil over medium-high heat and add the zucchini. Cook for 2 to 3 minutes, or until zucchini is translucent but not mushy. Remove from water and plunge immediately into a bowl of ice water. Drain and set aside.

Juice the lemon. Combine in a blender or food processor with coconut, hot water, olive oil and basil. Season with salt and pepper to taste. Process until smooth and toss with finished zucchini pasta. Serve over salad greens, topped with sweet potatoes.

American Taco Pie (GF, P, LC)

This Americanized Mexican dish is hearty and savory. It also freezes well in individual portions, making it an excellent choice for lunches or dinners on the go. Choose relatively lean ground beef, grass-fed if possible, for the best flavor.

Ingredients

1 ½ cups almond flour
¼ cup coconut oil
1 teaspoon salt
1 pound ground beef
1 tablespoon olive oil
1 medium onion
1 sweet red bell pepper
1 avocado
2 tablespoons grain-free taco seasoning
salt and pepper to taste

In a large bowl, mix the salt, coconut oil and almond flour, blending until a moldable dough forms. Transfer this dough to a standard pie plate and press into an even layer over the whole surface. In a large skillet, heat the olive oil to medium-high. Chop the onions and cook until softened and translucent. Add the ground beef and brown until completely cooked. Mix in the taco seasoning, salt and pepper. Cook for an addition two minutes and remove from heat. Pour the beef mixture into the pie plate and bake for 30 minutes at 350 degrees Fahrenheit, or until the crust is firm. Chop the lettuce, pepper and avocado roughly. Top the finished pie with vegetables and serve immediately.

Braised Chicken with Sweet Potatoes and Fennel Bulb (GF, P)

Chicken legs are inexpensive and flavorful, especially when combined with vitamin A-rich sweet potatoes and the unique taste of fennel. Don't be afraid of the amount of lemon juice required in this recipe; it helps brighten all the other tastes and adds a delightful natural tang that you shouldn't miss. For an extra touch, serve the chicken with a small curl of lemon peel as garnish.

4 chicken legs
2 cups chicken broth
3 medium sweet potatoes
1 bulb fennel
4 scallions
1 small head garlic
2 lemons
2 tablespoons coconut oil
salt and pepper to taste

Heat the coconut oil to medium high in a large skillet. Sear the chicken legs for about 5 minutes per side, or until lightly browned. Transfer to a large, oven-safe pot. Thinly slice the fennel and scallions. Mince the garlic and roughly chop the sweet potatoes. Reheat the skillet and add the fennel, cooking for about 5 minutes, or until the fennel is golden brown. Add the garlic and green onions, reduce heat, and cook for an additional 3 minutes or until the onions are wilted. Transfer the contents of the pan to the pot with the chicken. Juice the lemons and add the juice to the pot, along with the stock, salt and pepper. Cover and bake for 40 minutes at 300 degrees Fahrenheit, or until the chicken is cooked through and the sweet potatoes are tender.

Baked Cashew Chicken (GF, P, LC)

This Asian-inspired main dish is rich, sweet and flavorful. It also provides plenty of manganese, magnesium and copper, essential nutrients that many people lack. This meal is great if you need extra energy or you're cooking for a big group. Because of the fat in the cashews and coconut milk, this dish may separate when chilled. Just warm it up again and stir to restore the texture.

Ingredients

1 pound boneless, skinless chicken breast
2 cups water
1 cup cashews
½ cup coconut milk
¼ cup fresh mint
1 medium yellow onion
4 cloves garlic
1 lime
1-inch piece fresh ginger
2 tablespoons coconut oil
1 tablespoon ground coriander
1 tablespoon ground cumin seeds
1 teaspoon cinnamon
1 teaspoon cloves
salt and pepper to taste

Cut the onions into quarters and combine in a food processor with the cashews, ginger and garlic. Process until a soft puree forms and set aside. Heat the coconut oil in a medium pan over medium-high heat. Add the puree and stir-fry for about 5 minutes or until browned. Add the cumin, cloves, cinnamon and coriander and allow to cook for an additional 5 minutes, stirring periodically. Add the coconut milk and water. Season with salt and black pepper according to preference. Place the chicken in an oven-safe casserole dish and pour the coconut milk mixture over the meat. Cook at 300 degrees Fahrenheit for about 30 minutes, or until the chicken is cooked through. Serve with chopped mint and lime slices.

Savory Braised Duck (GF, P, LC)

Most people eat plenty of chicken and turkey, but very little duck. In fact, some have never enjoy this rich, flavorful bird! This simple braised recipe makes it easy to enjoy the nutrient-rich dark meat of this slightly unusual type of poultry. If duck is unavailable, you can substitute chicken thighs or similar cuts, but duck is definitely best. Allow the dish to rest for a little while after cooking to produce the tastiest finished product.

Ingredients

4 duck legs
1 cup duck or chicken stock
1 small head garlic
1 medium onion
1 stalk celery
2 medium carrots
1 ½ pounds tomatoes
1 small head broccoli
2 tablespoons flat-leaf parsley
1 tablespoon duck fat or coconut milk
1 tablespoon fresh thyme
salt and pepper to taste

Heat the duck fat or coconut oil in a large Dutch oven

over medium-high heat. Brown the duck legs, turning several times. Remove and set aside. Dice the garlic, onion, celery, carrots and tomatoes. Reheat the Dutch oven and sauté the vegetables in the remaining fat for about 5 minutes, or until tender. Return the duck legs to the pot and add the stock and thyme. Cook for approximately 90 minutes at about 325 degrees Fahrenheit, or until the carrots are soft and the duck is cooked through. Add the broccoli 15 minutes before the cooking process is done. Allow the meat to rest for 10 minutes, then serve garnished with parsley.

Stuffed Bell Peppers with Veal (GF, P, LC)

Ordinary stuffed peppers rely on conventionally-grown hamburger, but this version uses tender veal for a different taste and texture. To get the best results, look for pastured veal rather than crate-raised, since the texture of the meat is much better. Despite the lack of carbohydrates, this meal is extremely filling. Consider packing an extra pepper or two for lunch the next day!

Ingredients

1 pound ground veal
3 sweet red bell peppers
2 sweet orange bell peppers
3 tablespoons olive oil
1 medium red onion
½ pound cherry tomatoes
1 tablespoon fresh cilantro
1 tablespoon fresh oregano
1 tablespoon fresh marjoram
3 cloves garlic
salt and black pepper to taste

Remove the stems, ribs and seeds from all the bell peppers. Mince one red bell pepper and set aside. Cut the other four peppers in half, wash thoroughly, and arrange on a cooking dish, cut-side up. Brush with 1 tablespoon of olive oil and bake in a 350 degree oven for 20 minutes. Remove and set aside to cool.

In a separate pan, heat the remaining two tablespoons of olive oil to medium-high. Mince the garlic and onions and add to the pan, along with the minced red bell pepper. Saute for 2 minutes or until soft. Add the veal and season to taste using salt and black pepper. Cook, stirring occasionally, until the meat is done through. Add the fresh herbs and cherry tomatoes and continue cooking for an additional 2 minutes.
Stuff each pepper half with the meat mixture. Cover the entire pan with a sheet of aluminum foil or a lid and bake again for 25 minutes. Uncover and finish in the oven for an additional 10 minutes. Serve with a fresh salad.

No-Rice Pad Thai (GF, P, LC)

Pad Thai, the famous stir-fried noodle dish, is traditionally made with highly-refined rice noodles. This version uses mung bean noodles, which lack some of the health problems normally associated with rice. For a version that's lower in carbohydrates, consider substituting Japanese Shirataki noodles, which are made from a yam-like tuber and are about 97 percent water. While the basic recipe is vegetarian, it's easy to add in your favorite meat or seafood for a heartier version.

Ingredients

6 ounces dried mung bean noodles
1 large head broccoli
2 large onion
¼ cup peanuts or cashews
3 tablespoons coconut oil
4 scallions
3 cloves garlic
1 tablespoon sesame oil
1 tablespoon honey
1 teaspoon tamarind paste
1 teaspoon wheat-free tamari or fish sauce

Fill a large pot with water and bring to a boil over high

heat. Cook noodles according to package instructions, drain, and set aside. In a large wok or skillet heat the coconut oil to medium-high. Slice the onion, scallions and garlic. Stir fry the onion until lightly browned. Add the broccoli, breaking it up into individual florets. Stir fry until the broccoli turns bright green and becomes tender. Stir in garlic, followed by noodles. In a small bowl, combine sesame oil, tamarind paste, tamari and honey. Pour this mixture over the noodles and vegetable, stirring vigorously to prevent sticking and burning. Serve on individual plates garnished with scallions and crushed peanuts.

Baking and Desserts

Almond-coconut Chocolate Chip Cookies (GF, P)

Commercial chocolate chip cookies are loaded with preservatives, white flour, processed sugar and fillers. Even the kind you normally make at home require a number of heavily-processed, genetically modified
Ingredients
. Skip those unappealing cookies in favor of this recipe, which relies on natural sugars, almond flour and coconut flour to provide plenty of nutrition without the starch. Stick to store-bought almond flour to ensure proper lightness; the homemade variety can yield a very flat cookie.

Ingredients

5/8 cup almond flour
5 tablespoons unsalted butter
4 ounces grain-free dark chocolate
2 tablespoons honey or maple syrup
1 tablespoon coconut flour
1 large egg
1/3 teaspoon salt

¼ teaspoon vanilla extract

¼ teaspoon plain gelatin granules

¼ teaspoon baking soda

Bring butter to room temperature and combine with honey or syrup in a large bowl. Add gelatin, egg and vanilla. Allow the mixture to rest for 5 minutes. In a separate bowl, combine the almond and coconut flours, salt and baking soda. Add the dry ingredients to the wet mixture slowly, stirring continuously. Beat until combined. Chop chocolate into small pieces and stir into the cookie mixture. Line a baking pan with parchment paper. Scoop by teaspoonful's onto the pan, leaving plenty of space for the cookies to spread. Bake in a 350 degree Fahrenheit oven for 12 minutes, or until the edges brown slightly. Eat warm with a glass of your favorite dairy or plant milk.

Honey-Buttermilk Panna Cotta (GF, P*, LC**)

Traditional panna cotta is naturally grain free, making it a great substitute for commercial puddings laden with corn starch. This version uses buttermilk for extra flavor and natural maple sweeteners. Whenever possible, stick to using real vanilla beans, which provide a more subtle and interesting taste than extracts. Enjoy this rich and appealing recipe with plenty of fresh raspberries or strawberries.

1 ½ cups natural buttermilk
1 cup heavy cream
1/3 cup maple syrup
1 tablespoon warm water
2 ¼ teaspoons plain gelatin granules
1/2 vanilla bean or 1 teaspoon vanilla extract

Combine the gelatin with 1 tablespoon of warm water in a small bowl. Allow to stand for 10 minutes. In a medium saucepan, heat the cream and maple syrup to medium, whisking continuously to prevent curdling. Allow the mixture to steam slightly, then remove from the heat and allow to cool for five minutes. Whisk in the gelatin mixture until all granules have dissolved completely. Slit the vanilla bean and scrape the contents into the gelatin-cream mixture. Add buttermilk, whisking until the mixture is smooth and creamy. Pour into one large pan or six individual bowls. Refrigerate until firm, 6 hours or more.

*The cream and buttermilk make this recipe unsuitable for paleo dieters.

** Replace the maple syrup with your favorite non-caloric sweeteners to reduce the carbohydrate count of this dessert.

No-Grain Sandwich Bread (GF, P, LC)

Going grain-free doesn't mean saying goodbye to sandwiches, French toast, bread pudding or stuffing, as long as you know how to use your ingredients. This bread is gluten free and filled with nutrient-dense foods, so you'll be surprised at how satisfying it can be. Fluffy, nutty and light, this bread is everything you dreamed grain-free eating could be!

Ingredients

1 3/4 cups almond flour
5 eggs
¼ cup flax seed meal
1/8 cup coconut flour
1 ¾ tablespoons coconut oil
1 tablespoon vinegar
1 tablespoon honey or date paste
1 teaspoon baking soda
¼ teaspoon salt

In a large bowl, combine the almond and coconut flours, flax meal, baking soda and salt. In a separate bowl, whisk together the eggs, coconut oil, vinegar and honey. Pour the wet ingredients into the dry mixture, stirring continuously until just combined. Grease a medium loaf pan and pour the batter in, spreading with a spatula if necessary. Bake at 350 degrees Fahrenheit for 30 minutes or until the top of the loaf browns lightly and the center is firm. Allow to cool and serve.

Banana Coconut Muffins (GF, P, LC)

These muffins are a delicious treat after dinner or for a quick breakfast on a workday. Their flavor improves a day or so after baking, so don't be afraid to make extra and store them in your refrigerator. The bananas and dates provide plenty of sweetness, so there's no reason to add more carbohydrate-heavy options. If you are in the very-low-carbohydrate phase of a low carb diet, however, these muffins may not be suitable. Try them with a little coconut oil or softened butter, or eat them on their own.

Ingredients

6 large eggs
3 large bananas
¾ cup coconut flour
½ cup walnuts
5 tablespoons coconut milk
¼ cup coconut oil
2 tablespoons dates
1 tablespoon hot water
2 ½ teaspoons baking powder
½ teaspoon lemon juice
1 teaspoon salt

Soak the dates in the hot water for 10 minutes, then mash with a fork. Combine in a large bowl with the eggs, coconut milk, lemon juice and salt. Stir in coconut oil and set aside. Sift the baking soda and coconut flour into a medium bowl, then stir the dry ingredients slowly into the liquid ones. Mix until no lumps are visible and the ingredients are well mixed.

Peel and mash the bananas, then fold them into the muffin mixture until completely combined. Stir in walnuts. Scoop into a greased 12-cup muffin pan and bake at 400 degrees Fahrenheit for 18 to 20 minutes. Remove from oven and allow to cool for 10 minutes, then release from pan with the tip of a butter knife and enjoy.

No-flour Chocolate Lava Cake (GF, P)

If you're looking for the perfect holiday dessert indulgence without a trace of grains, this chocolate lava cake is the perfect choice. It includes dark chocolate, which is known for its healthy antioxidants, as well as natural sweeteners. To make ahead, follow the recipe recommendations up to the baking step, then freeze the entire tin and bring to room temperature about a half hour before you bake the cake.

Ingredients

½ pound unsweetened baking chocolate
2/3 cup unsalted butter or coconut oil
2/3 cup honey
6 egg yolks
3 egg whites

Combine the chocolate and butter or coconut oil in a heavy-bottomed pot over low heat. In a separate bowl, beat the honey and egg yolks until they are creamy, thick and fluffy. Add the chocolate mixture directly to the egg yolk mixture and beat vigorously for 5 to 10 minutes or until well combined. In a separate container, beat the egg whites until they become frothy and develop stiff peaks. Fold the meringue into the chocolate mixture carefully until just combined. Grease 6 individual ramekins and divide the batter between them. Bake in a 425 degree Fahrenheit oven for 5 to 7 minutes, or until the center is hot and liquid but the edges are solid. Serve hot with your favorite ice cream or frozen yogurt.

Coconut-vanilla Frozen Dessert (GF, P, LC)

If you read the ingredients on your favorite ice cream package, you may be surprised by how many grain products and fillers it includes. Homemade recipes are often grain-free, but they still rely on refined sugars and other ingredients that tend to be unhealthy. This recipe produces a great-tasting frozen dessert you can make at home without an ice cream maker, plus it's low in carbohydrates and paleo diet-friendly!

Ingredients

2 cups coconut milk
2 large eggs
2 vanilla beans or 4 tablespoons vanilla extract
3 tablespoons raw honey or equivalent no-calorie sweetener

Slit the vanilla beans and scrape them thoroughly. Combine the vanilla scrapings with the coconut milk in a double boiler and heat over low heat until steaming. Add the honey or no-calorie sweetener and stir until dissolved. In a separate bowl, whisk the eggs until they are fluffy and thick. Ladle 1/3 to ½ cup of the hot coconut milk mixture into the eggs, whisking vigorously to combine. Repeat the process, then add the egg mixture to the remainder of the coconut milk mixture.

Whisk for 2 to 3 minutes, or until a thick, smooth custard has formed. Remove from heat and allow the custard to cool to room temperature, then transfer to the refrigerator for at least an hour. Pour the custard into a large baking dish and place in the freezer for about 2 hours or until completely set. Stir vigorously to break up the ice once every 15 to 30 minutes. Remove this dessert from the freezer 10 minutes before serving.

Almond Flour Blueberry Muffins (GF, P, LC*)

This classic snack and breakfast favorite is remarkably simple. It substitutes almond flour for the standard white flour, and natural honey for refined sugar. You'll enjoy the traditional taste, smell and texture of these delicious muffins, whether you eat them fresh out of the oven or save a few for snacking. If your diet doesn't permit use of dairy, consider substituting a grain free soy or coconut yogurt instead.

Ingredients

2 ½ cups almond flour
1 cup fresh blueberries
4 tablespoons butter or coconut milk
2 eggs
1/3 cup honey
1/3 cup yogurt
½ vanilla bean or 1 teaspoon vanilla extract
¼ teaspoon nutmeg
¼ teaspoon cinnamon
¼ teaspoon salt

Combine all ingredients other than the blueberries in a large bowl or food processor and beat until well combined. Fold in the blueberries carefully. Grease a 12 cup muffin tin and divide the mixture between the cups. Bake in a 325 degree Fahrenheit oven for 15 to 20 minutes or until the centers have set.

*To make this recipe lower in carbohydrates, substitute your favorite no-calorie sweetener and an equivalent amount of liquid to replace the honey.

Cinnamon Roll Muffins (GF, P)

Regular cinnamon rolls rely on the gluten found in wheat flour to produce their springy texture and flaky interiors. This muffin recipe duplicates the flavors of cinnamon rolls in muffin form, but it uses no grains. You'll love the rich but healthy taste of their cinnamon topping and the moist interior of these delightful treats.

Ingredients

1 cup almond flour
¼ cup grapeseed oil
¼ cup agave nectar or maple syrup
1/8 cup coconut flour
3 eggs
1 tablespoon vanilla extract
½ teaspoon baking soda
¼ teaspoon salt
Topping
1/8 cup agave nectar or maple syrup
1 tablespoon coconut oil
1 tablespoon cinnamon

In a medium bowl, combine the flours, salt and baking soda. In a separate large bowl, blend the agave nectar or maple syrup, oil, vanilla extract and eggs. Slowly pour the dry ingredients into the wet mixture, stirring carefully until there are no lumps. Grease a 12 cup muffin tin and spoon batter into the cups. In a small bowl, blend the agave, coconut oil and cinnamon. Divide this mixture between the muffin cups and bake at 350 degrees Fahrenheit for 8 to 12 minutes or until the centers are solid.

Almond Biscuits (GF, P, LC)

These biscuits have a crisp but crumbly texture and provide plenty of protein. They're great as a part of any breakfast, but they also make an excellent addition to Thanksgiving menus, brunches, dinners and much more. To decrease the carbohydrates in this recipe, simply omit the honey.

Ingredients

2 ½ cups almond flour
2 eggs
¼ cup coconut oil
1 tablespoon honey
½ teaspoon baking soda
½ teaspoon salt

In a medium bowl, combine the almond flour, soda and salt. In a separate large bowl, blend the eggs, honey and coconut oil. Pour the dry ingredient mixture into the oil mixture, stirring continuously to produce a moldable dough. Place the dough on a piece of parchment paper and cover with an additional piece, then roll out to about 1 ½ inches in thickness. If necessary, dust the dough with additional almond flour.

Using a biscuit cutter or large mouthed glass, cut the

dough into 10 biscuits, rerolling as necessary. Line a baking sheet with parchment paper. Transfer the uncooked biscuits to the sheet using a spatula and bake at 350 degrees Fahrenheit for 15 minutes, or until the bottoms of the biscuits begin to brown. Serve hot with gravy, jam or any other food.

Rye-style Flax Bread (GF, P, LC)

While a basic sandwich bread works for most uses, not every meal is appropriate for it. That's where a stronger-tasting option can help. This flax seed-based bread has the same color and general flavor as traditional rye bread, but it lacks the potentially-damaging health problems that come with that great. Eat this bread plain, toasted, or as part of your favorite sandwich. To reduce the bread's carbohydrate content, simply omit the honey or replace it with your favorite no-calorie sweetener.

Ingredients

1 cup almond flour
¾ cup ground flax seed
3 eggs
¼ cup water
2 tablespoons extra virgin olive oil
2 tablespoons caraway seeds
1 teaspoon honey
¾ teaspoon lemon juice
½ teaspoon baking soda
½ teaspoon salt
Coconut oil
Combine the ground flax seed, soda, salt and almond

flour in a large bowl. In a separate small bowl, mix the honey, water, eggs, oil and lemon juice. Slowly stir the wet ingredients into the dry mixture to form a thick batter, then add caraway seeds and mix until evenly distributed. Allow the batter to rest for 5 minutes. Grease a mini loaf pan with coconut oil and fill with the batter. Bake for 30 minutes at 350 degrees Fahrenheit, or until the center is solid. Allow the bread to cool, slice and serve.

Snacks

Homemade Yogurt (GF, P, LC*)

Whether you prefer traditional dairy yogurt or you're going milk-free, yogurt is an important staple that any grain-free cook can't do without. It's essential in many baking recipes and makes a delicious meat marinade, as well as a snack on its own. Many commercial yogurts contain large amounts of fillers, sugars and other grain-derived ingredients, making them inappropriate for all kinds of diets. Making your own allows you to control what's in your yogurt and lets you produce the perfect texture for your preferences.

Ingredients

4 cups milk, cream or coconut milk
1 tablespoon honey
1 package powdered yogurt starter

Bring the milk, coconut or cream to a boil in a large pot over high heat. Immediately remove from stove and cool to room temperature. Remove 1/2 cup of the liquid to a small separate bowl and combine with the packaged starter. Mix well, then return the starter mixture to the main bowl. Combine thoroughly and pour into a yogurt maker. Ferment for 24 to 30 hours, then remove to the refrigerator to thicken. If desired, strain the yogurt through cheesecloth suspended over a bowl to produce thicker, "Greek-style" yogurt.

*To reduce carbohydrates, omit the honey from dairy-based yogurt. This recipe relies on some sugar for successful fermentation, so no-calorie sweetener is not appropriate.

Roasted Pumpkin Seeds (GF, P, LC)

These pumpkin seeds with sweet spices are the perfect snack for the autumn holidays. Save the seeds from your jack-o-lantern or pie pumpkins to produce this simple but fragrant food. They're a great substitute for grain-based crackers and unhealthy chips.

Ingredients

½ cup fresh pumpkin seeds
1 tablespoon olive oil
½ teaspoon ginger powder
¼ teaspoon salt
¼ teaspoon allspice
¼ teaspoon cinnamon
1/8 teaspoon cardamom
1/8 teaspoon cloves
1/8 teaspoon black pepper

In a medium bowl, toss the oil with the pumpkin seeds. In a separate small bowl, combine the powdered spices and stir well. Pour over the seed mixture and stir thoroughly to coat. Bake on an ungreased cookie sheet at 375 degrees Fahrenheit or until fragrant and well-toasted. Eat while still warm or allow to cool. Store in an air-tight container.

Coconut Chicken Strips (GF, P, LC)

Coconut and chicken are a great combination, and this recipe gives you an alternative to grain-heavy fried snacking options. This baked, non-battered chicken recipe is delicious and a lot of fun to eat, whether it's as a snack or part of a special dinner. Try it with salad, guacamole, or a basic coleslaw recipe.

Ingredients

1 pound boneless, skinless chicken breasts
1 cup plain shredded coconut
½ cup coconut flour
2 eggs
1 tablespoon coconut milk
1 teaspoon garlic powder
½ teaspoon sharp paprika
salt and black pepper to taste

Flatten the chicken breasts with a mallet or rolling pin to an even thickness. Cut the meat into long pieces approximately 1 inch wide. Combine the eggs, coconut milk, salt and pepper in one small bowl. Beat vigorously until completely mixed. In a separate small bowl, mix the coconut flour, garlic powder and paprika. Place the coconut shreds in a third small bowl.

Working quickly, coat each strip first in coconut flour, then in the egg mixture. Roll the coated strips in shredded coconut and place on a large, ungreased baking sheet. Leave approximately 1 inch between strips. Bake for about 10 minutes at 400 degrees Fahrenheit, or until the chicken is cooked through completely. Eat plain or serve with homemade grain-free plum or sweet and sour sauce.

Fruit and Nut-Stuffed Pears (GF, P, LC)

Baked pears with sweet spices, rich nuts and fresh fruit is an excellent way to give yourself an energy boost without turning to crackers or cookies. This recipe is natural, healthy, and appropriate for most diets. Very low-carb dieters may find the sugars in the fruit to be excessive, but most should be able to eliminate the honey and still enjoy this treat.

Ingredients

4 fat, flat-bottomed pears
¼ pound red grapes
¼ cup natural apple juice
2 tablespoons honey
½ cup sliced almonds
½ lemon
1 teaspoon cinnamon

In a small bowl, combine 1 tablespoon of honey with the sliced almonds. Line a baking sheet or pie plate with parchment paper. Bake the almonds on top of the parchment at 300 degrees Fahrenheit for 15 or 20 minutes, or until crisp. Core the pears from the top, leaving the bottom solid. Place the pears on a separate pie plate, cored ends up. Dice the grapes and place them in a small bow. Combine the almond mixture with the grapes and stuff the pears. Juice the lemon and combine it with the apple juice, remaining honey and cinnamon in a small bowl. Pour this mixture into the stuffed cores and all around each piece of fruit. Bake at 300 degrees Fahrenheit for 30 minutes, or until the pears are tender and fully-cooked.

Sesame Almond Crackers (GF, P, LC)

Chips and crackers make for appealing snacking, but their high percentage of grains and other unhealthy carbohydrates can be damaging to your body. That's why these buttery or coconut-flavored seed-based crackers are such a good alternative. You'll get that savory, crunchy experience you've been craving without the grain.

Ingredients

¾ cup almond flour
2 tablespoons butter or coconut oil
1 egg white
1 tablespoon sesame seeds
3/8 teaspoon salt
¼ teaspoon onion powder
¼ teaspoon garlic powder

Beat the egg white until frothy. Allow the butter to soften at room temperature. In a small bowl, combine all dry ingredients, then blend in egg white and butter until a soft dough forms. Chill for 30 minutes, then drop by ¼ teaspoons onto a baking sheet lined with parchment. Leave 1 inch or more between dough balls. Cover with parchment paper or plastic wrap and flatten to about 1/16 inch thick. Prick with a fork and bake for 20 minutes at 325 degrees Fahrenheit, or until golden brown. Allow to cool and store in an airtight container.

Cheese Crisps (GF, P*, LC)

Crispy, crunchy and composed entirely of cheese, these unique little snacks are a grain-free dieter's snacking salvation. They're low in carbohydrates and high in flavor, making them a satisfying choice for between-meal treats. Try several different kinds of cheese to make a variety mix. Plus, these simple crisps can be made in the microwave!

Ingredients

8 ounce bag shredded cheddar, mozzarella, Swiss or Monterey jack cheese
garlic powder or onion powder to taste (optional)

Line a microwaveable plate or tray with parchment paper. Place 1 tablespoon of shredded cheese in the middle of the plate and spread it out into an even layer approximately 3 inches across. Microwave on high for 30 seconds. Remove the paper and crisp from the plate and allow it to cool, then peel the paper off of the crisp. Repeat using the same piece of parchment paper. When all crisps are cool, store in an air-tight container. For longer storage, try the freezer.

*Paleo dieters may need to eat these in moderation, as

some diets restrict dairy.

Chicken Cracklings (GF, P, LC)

These meaty snacks may sound a little unusual at first, but they'll soon grow on you. They're made using the same theory as pork rinds, but without the pig. The result is salty, meaty and surprisingly low in "bad" fats. This recipe is also great for using the skin from chicken thigh recipes that require skinless meat.

Ingredients

Skin from 8 pre-roasted chicken thighs
Salt and pepper to taste

Cut the pieces of skin into pieces a few inches across and spread them in a single layer on a large baking sheet. Avoid stacking the skins, as this can prevent crisping. Season lightly with salt on one side and bake for 30 minutes at 350 degrees Fahrenheit. Flip the skin and bake an additional 10 minutes, or until crisp and brown. Eat immediately or allow the cracklings to cool and store in the refrigerator. Reheat before serving.

Salads, Soups and Sides

Creamy Cauliflower Soup (GF, P, LC)

This rich and delicious soup makes a great substitute for potato or grain-based soups on a chilly day. It's also egg free, for diets that limit egg consumption. Substitute vegetable stock for the chicken stock to make this dish vegetarian-friendly for larger gatherings or guests.

1 head cauliflower
2 quarts chicken stock
1 large onion
¼ cup milk
2 tablespoons olive oil
1 teaspoons them
salt and pepper to taste

Chop the onion and the cauliflower. Mince the garlic. Heat the olive oil in a large pot over medium heat and sauté the onion and garlic for 5 minutes, or until translucent. Add the stock, thyme and cauliflower, then bring to a boil over high heat. Reduce to a simmer and cook until the cauliflower almost dissolves. Puree in a blender until completely smooth, then season with salt and pepper as desired. Serve hot, garnished with thyme.

Matzoh Ball Soup (GF, P, LC)

This traditional Passover soup is also beloved by plenty of non-Jewish cooks. It's known as a health-boosting remedy for cold or flu, but the wheat-based matzoh it requires is off-limits for grain-free diets. This version uses almond flour instead of wheat flour to produce surprisingly authentic-tasting matzoh balls. Whether you'd like a wheat-free substitute for your Passover table or you just love chicken soup, this recipe will soon be staple of your cookbook. To render the soup vegetarian-friendly, simply substitute vegetable broth instead of chicken.

Ingredients

6 cups chicken stock
2 cups almond flour
4 eggs
2 teaspoons salt
pepper to taste

Combine eggs, salt and pepper in a medium bowl, beating vigorously. Slowly add the almond flour, stirring continuously to produce a soft dough. Refrigerate for at least 2 hours and set aside. Boil a large pot of water over high heat and drop the batter by tablespoons-full into the boiling liquid. Reduce heat to low, cover, and allow to simmer for 20 minutes. Remove with a slotted spoon. In a separate pot, heat 6 cups chicken stock to a simmer. Gently place the finished matzoh balls into the stock and heat for an additional 10 minutes. Serve hot, with at least 2 to 3 matzoh balls per bowl.

Split Pea and Mushroom Soup (GF)

This hearty soup provides protein in the form of mushrooms and split peas, savory flavors from stock, garlic and onion, and a little spice in the form of paprika. This recipe contains no meat, but if you'd like more of a meaty flavor, substitute chicken or beef stock for the vegetable broth. Like many hearty soups, this recipe is actually best the next day.

Ingredients

1 quart vegetable broth
3 cups water
1 cup split yellow peas
½ pound mushrooms
1 cup kale
2 tablespoons olive oil
2 cloves garlic
1 small onion
2 bay leaves
½ teaspoon smoked paprika
salt and black pepper to taste

Combine bay leaves, split peas, water and paprika in a medium pan. Bring to a boil over high heat, then reduce to low and simmer until the peas fall apart. Remove from heat and set aside. Discard bay leaves. Chop onions, kale and garlic. In a large pan, heat the olive oil to medium-low and sauté chopped onion. Slice the mushrooms and add to the pan with the garlic and kale. Cook until tender and set aside. Remove bay leaf from split peas. Combine pea mixture with mushroom mixture along with stock. Cook for 30 minutes or until thick and well combined. Serve hot.

Squash Oven Fries (GF, P, LC)

Even for potato eaters, conventional fries tend to be off-limits for a grain-free diet because of the risk that they have been cooked in corn oil. These lower-carbohydrate substitutes are made from squash, cooked in olive oil, and made right in your home oven. They're crisp and much healthier. Choose them as a side for your next batch of barbecue chicken or even to go with your morning eggs.

Ingredients

1 large butternut squash or pumpkin
¼ cup olive oil
1 tablespoon dried oregano
salt and black pepper to taste

Cut the squash in half lengthwise and remove the seeds. Peel the outside and cut the meat into sticks of your preferred size. Place the squash fries in a large bowl and toss them with the olive oil, then the spices. Season to taste with salt and pepper. Place in a single layer on a large cookie sheet and roast at 425 degrees Fahrenheit for 20 minutes, or until the outside is crisp.

Cranberry Steak Salad (GF, P, LC)

This salad is hearty enough to be a meal in and of itself. It uses skirt steak, which is not normally considered a tender or appealing cut, but careful preparation helps bring out the incredible flavors of this meat. When combined with fresh cranberries and fennel, it produces a fresh salad that's affordable and delicious. If fresh cranberries are unavailable in your area, consider substituting frozen.

1 pound skirt steak
2 cups arugula
1 large bulb fennel
½ cup fresh cranberries
2 scallions
1 tablespoon olive oil
1 tablespoon fresh thyme
1 tablespoon fresh basil
1 bunch flat leaf parsley
salt and pepper to taste
3 tablespoons of your favorite vinaigrette

Fill a small pot with water and bring it to a boil over high heat. Add the cranberries and cook for about 5 minutes, or until the berries soften. Drain and set aside to cool. Season the steak with salt and black pepper to taste, then sprinkle thoroughly with basil and thyme. Heat the coconut oil in a large skillet over medium-high heat and add the steak. Cook, flipping frequently throughout the process, until the steak reaches your preferred level of doneness. Transfer to a plate or cutting board and allow to rest for 5 minutes.

Slice the fennel thinly and combine in a large bowl with the cranberries and arugula. Cut the steak into thin slices and toss with the vegetables. Serve topped with your favorite dressing and garnish with parsley.

Spinach and Blood Orange Salad (GF, P)

Light and refreshing, this salad is a delicious starter or small meal. The fruit adds tartness and sweetness, while the spinach provides plenty of important minerals. Combined with honey and almonds, this recipe is a great meatless addition to just about any meal. If you can't obtain blood oranges, consider substituting Meyer lemons or sweet pink grapefruit.

Ingredients

½ cup spinach leaves
2 medium blood oranges
1 sweet pear
½ cup slivered or chopped almonds
¼ cup dried, unsweetened cranberries
1 tablespoon honey
Dressing
½ cup olive oil
2 tablespoons rice vinegar
1 teaspoon prepared brown mustard
salt and pepper to taste

In a small bowl, combine the honey with the almonds. Line a baking sheet with parchment paper and spread the almonds over it. Bake at 300 degrees Fahrenheit for

15 to 20 minutes or until browned. Remove and set aside.

In a separate bowl, combine the olive oil, rice vinegar, mustard, salt and pepper. Whisk vigorously to combine and set aside. Cut the pear and citrus fruit into large pieces. Combine in a large bowl with the spinach and dried cranberries. Pour the vinaigrette over the entire salad and toss. Serve garnished with honeyed almonds.

Kale Coleslaw (GF, P, LC)

Traditional cabbage coleslaw is perfectly appropriate for a grain-free diet, as long as you can ensure that the dressing includes no dextrose or other grain-derived ingredients. This recipe provides a little extra punch, however. It includes nutrient-dense kale and almonds, making it much healthier than the standard fare.

Ingredients

2 large bunches kale
1 pound carrots
2 scallions
½ cup olive oil
½ cup coconut oil
¼ cup chopped almonds
2 egg yolks
1 tablespoon lemon juice
1 tablespoon prepared mustard
salt and pepper to taste

Cut the kale and scallions into thin strips. Shred the carrots and toss with the kale mixture. Mix in the almonds, stirring carefully. Mix the olive and coconut oils together in a small pan or microwaveable bowl and heat until just melted. In a small bowl, combine the egg yolks, mustard and 1 teaspoon of the lemon juice. Whisk vigorously, dripping the melted oils in slowly to create an emulsion. Stabilize the bowl with a cloth or towel if necessary. When the dressing reaches the desired consistency, add the remaining lemon juice. Season with salt and pepper. Add 2 or 3 tablespoons of dressing to the kale mixture and stir to coat. Refrigerate and serve cold.

Roasted Winter Squash (GF, P, LC)

This simple side dish is tasty and appropriate for a wide range of diet restrictions. It's gluten-free, contains no dairy, and also lacks meat. Some low-carbohydrate diets prohibit winter squash, but this mildly-sweet dish should be appropriate for the later stages of these eating plans. Enjoy roasted squash as a side with your favorite meats or on its own as a light meal.

Ingredients

1 acorn squash or 2 delicata squash
¼ cup olive or coconut oil
1 teaspoon cinnamon
salt and pepper to taste

Cut the squash in half lengthwise and remove the stems, seeds and membranes. Place cut side down on a cutting board and cut into slices about ¼ inch thick. Lay in a single layer on a large cookie sheet, leaving space between each piece. Drizzle with 1/8 cup oil, then sprinkle with salt, pepper and cinnamon. Bake at 400 degrees Fahrenheit for 10 minutes, or until golden brown. Flip, drizzle with the remaining oil, and bake for an additional 5 minutes. Serve hot.

A 5-Day Grain Free Meal Plan

This sample grain free meal plan is designed to help you get an idea of the best way to go grain free. It is not oriented toward any one type of diet, however. That means that if you need to avoid specific ingredients, it may be necessary to modify the meal plan slightly. Use this diet plan as a springboard for your new way of cooking, rather than an exact set of rules. After all, there's nothing to limit you other than your imagination!

Day 1

Breakfast: Hot Porridge, orange juice

Lunch: Cranberry Steak Salad

Snack: Cheese Crisps, sliced pears

Dinner: Braised Chicken with Sweet Potatoes and Fennel Bulb, Spinach and Blood Orange Salad

Day 2

Breakfast: Green Eggs, Rye-style Flax Bread

Lunch: Split Pea and Mushroom Soup

Snack: Homemade Yogurt

Dinner: Stuffed Bell Peppers with Veal, Kale Coleslaw

Day 3

Breakfast: Banana Coconut Muffins

Lunch: American Taco Pie

Snack: Cinnamon Roll Muffins

Dinner: Pot Roast with Fresh Vegetables, Almond Biscuits

Day 4

Breakfast: Sweet Potato Breakfast Casserole

Lunch: Roasted Winter Squash, Coconut Chicken Strips

Snack: Fruit and Nut-Stuffed Pears

Dinner: Creamy Cauliflower Soup, Barbecue Chicken with Grain-free Sauce

Day 5

Breakfast: Almond Waffles, orange juice, Homemade Yogurt

Lunch: Baked Cashew Chicken

Snack: Roasted Pumpkin Seeds

Dinner: Zucchini Pasta with Roasted Sweet Potatoes and Coconut Pesto, Squash Oven Fries, Coconut-vanilla Frozen Dessert

Conclusion

There's no reason to feel like eating grain-free has to be a limitation. The world is full of fantastic and healthy grain-free recipes that are suitable for paleo dieters, celiacs and other with wheat sensitivities, and low-carb eating plans. If you just take a little bit of time to think about all the options, you'll be surprised by all the great things you can eat. While it can be difficult living in a wheat and corn-obsessed world, you won't be in danger of going hungry. All you have to do with learn to think outside the grain-based box.

These recipes provide a starting place for anyone who wants to enjoy their food without worrying about the health problems that grains and other carbohydrates could be causing. It's time to stop suffering from headaches, digestive problems, nutritional deficiencies and all the other issues that modern grains can induce. The alternatives are rich, delicious and extremely healthy. Try a new no-grain recipe today!

www.ingramcontent.com/pod-product-compliance
Lightning Source LLC
LaVergne TN
LVHW021714060526
838200LV00050B/2651